PRESIDENT FROM MISSOURI

Harry S. Truman

by RALPH G. MARTIN

On April 12, 1945, President Franklin D. Roosevelt died in office and the attention of the world was focused on his successor, Harry Truman. No president has ever assumed office with such an awesome burden of responsibilities. The United States was embroiled in the worst war in history, and Truman had to make decisions affecting the lives and destinies of millions of people. He confounded all skeptics with the astuteness and vigor he displayed in coping with the problems, both domestic and foreign, that confronted him.

Truman's early years in Missouri were rich with the heritage of rural America, the life of hard work and common sense, and of forthright words between men. He served with distinction as an artillery captain in World War I, then became active in county politics and dreamed of one day being a congressman.

When Truman was elected to the Senate in 1934, he was attacked by the press as a tool of the Pendergast political machine that supported him. But he answered this challenge with his vigorous campaign for re-election in 1940, a victory he won exclusively on his own merits. After he assumed the Presidency, he launched such notable programs as the Truman Doctrine, the Marshall Plan, NATO, the Point Four Program—all in an effort to build a peace that would endure. He was often outspoken and made enemies. The press frequently vilified him. But again it was the people who vindicated him by re-electing him to office in the famous campaign of 1948, a race Thomas Dewey was predicted to win with ease.

Harry Truman could be stubborn as well as resilient, and the author has captured the spirit of the man—his mixture of toughness and good will, cockiness and humility, deep loyalty to friends and honesty to all. He was proud to be called a common man, but history shows the least common of all.

Jacket by RUPERT

PRESIDENT
FROM MISSOURI

Harry S. Truman

On April 12, 1945, President Franklin D. Roosevelt died in office and the attention of the world was focused on his successor, Harry S. Truman. No president has ever assumed office with such an awesome burden of responsibilities. But he confounded all skeptics with the astuteness and vigor he displayed in coping with the staggering problems, both domestic and foreign, that confronted him. He launched such notable and successful programs as the Truman Doctrine, the Marshall Plan, the Point Four Program, NATO—all to build a peace that would endure. The author has captured the spirit of the man—his mixture of toughness and good will, cockiness and humility, deep loyalty to friends and honesty to all. He was proud to be called a common man, but history shows that he was one of the least common of all.

PRESIDENT FROM MISSOURI

☆　☆　☆　☆　☆

Harry S. Truman

by

Ralph G. Martin

Published simultaneously in the United States and Canada
by Julian Messner
A Division of Simon & Schuster, Inc.
1 West 39 Street, New York, N.Y. 10018

Copyright, © 1964 by Ralph G. Martin

Fourth Printing, 1966

Printed in the United States of America
Library of Congress Catalog Card No. 61-20154

JULIAN MESSNER
NEW YORK

Published simultaneously in the United States and Canada
By Julian Messner
A Division of Simon & Schuster, Inc.
1 West 39 Street, New York, N.Y. 10018

Copyright, © 1964 by Ralph G. Martin

Fourth printing, 1966

Printed in the United States of America
Library of Congress Catalog Card No. 64-20154

For my three dear children—Maury, Betsy and Tina

PRESIDENT
FROM MISSOURI

Harry S. Truman

HE WAS A SMALL BOY WITH THICK GLASSES, a shy boy who usually stood and watched the other eight-year-olds play ball, and seldom played with them. He was usually neat and obedient, and the other boys quietly thought of Harry as a "sissy" because he knew how to cook and never once got into a fist fight. And it didn't help him any when they saw him carrying a big leather music portfolio under his arm when he went to take his daily piano lesson.

Still, when they played cops and robbers and got all mixed up about Jesse James and his brother Frank, and the Dalton Brothers and Wyatt Earp, it was Harry they called in to straighten them out. He told them it was Frank James who had spent some time in their home town jail of Independence; that it was the Dalton Brothers who were recently shot and killed in Kansas, and that Wyatt Earp had been the sheriff in Lamar, another Missouri town.

When they played baseball and got into hot arguments about who was safe and who was out, they would usually call on Harry to be their umpire. Somtimes, but not often, they even let him play.

The reason Harry S. Truman was a boy of books rather

than baseball was because he could barely see without his glasses. He had a flat eyeball and it seriously limited his sight. Since glasses were expensive, and not many boys wore them in those days, his mother discouraged him from roughhousing with the other boys, and so he turned to books.

Everybody said he was "old for his years" (probably because he learned to read when he was five, and always seemed so serious), and the women usually pointed him out as "a model boy." But some of them changed their minds when Harry took his younger brother Vivian for a ride and dumped him into a mud hole. Or, another time, when he was caught cutting off his brother's hair.

Those early days were full of great adventures for young Harry Truman. His father bought him a beautiful, black Shetland pony and he would ride alongside his father all over their big farm of some six hundred acres. Once he fell off his pony and his father made him walk the rest of the way home to teach him a lesson. The lesson stuck. He never fell off again.

Harry watched the wheat harvest and the threshing, the corn shucking and the mowing and the stacking of hay. He had a small black-and-tan dog named Tandy and a bob-tailed Maltese gray cat, Bob, and the three of them would often hunt field mice together.

Somehow, he seemed to have more accidents than his brother or his sister Mary Jane or anybody else in the family. Once he swallowed a peach pit and almost choked to death. And another time he fell and broke his collarbone. When his brother had a minor case of diphtheria, Harry, who was also stricken, was so ill that his arms and legs were paralyzed for months.

All this gave his father the idea that Harry was "more delicate" than Vivian. Even though he taught Harry how to handle the mules and hogs, the sheep and cattle, it was Vivian he took with him when he went to town on his animal-trading business.

Independence then was more than just another town. It had been the jumping-off place for all those settlers in their covered wagons heading west for a new life—or gold. The first overland mail stagecoach lines started from there. Some Civil War skirmishes took place there, and the city was held twice by Confederate troops, each time for only one day before the Union troops recaptured it. Later, cowboys passed through town on their way with their herds of cattle to the big city markets.

During the days that Harry was growing up, Independence stayed a small town and nearby Kansas City became the important place. Missouri itself had changed from a frontier state to a farming state. The fur trappers moved on to wilder areas, the steamboat traffic was largely replaced by railroads, the plantations were broken up into smaller farms and tenant farmers replaced the slaves.

All four of Harry Truman's grandparents came from Kentucky and migrated to Missouri. The earliest known Truman had come from England where the family had built a big brewery in 1665, and the next Truman to come to America settled in New London, Connecticut, as a carpenter, and was later elected constable. But in the Truman family record, the first entry reads: "Anderson S. Truman was borned February the 27th, 1816." He was Harry Truman's grandfather, a former school director who settled on a farm in Jackson County, Missouri. His middle name was Shippe.

11

Harry Truman remembers seeing this grandfather stretched out in bed, still and stiff, while his aunts were crying, and recalls how he pulled at his grandfather's beard, trying to wake him.

But Harry best remembered his other grandfather, Solomon Young, who took him to the fair when he was six, and bought him striped candy and peanuts. Solomon Young was a man of a different cut. He knew men and mules and was a businessman and a trader. Dignified-looking, a handsome man with a full beard, Grandfather Young set up a freighting business of Conestoga wagons with ox teams, taking them from Missouri to Salt Lake City to San Francisco. In those days that was a six-month round trip. The gold rush was still a fever, the Indians still a danger, and a Civil War had divided the North and the South.

On one of his trips, Young ran a herd of fifteen hundred head of cattle through wild Indian country and lost five hundred on the way. In wide-eyed grandson Harry, Solomon Young had a ready audience for all his western adventures.

Grandmother Young had similar stories of high drama that she served grandson Harry along with her delicious homemade peach butter and cookies and apple pie. Her most retold story, one that always fascinated Harry, occurred at the start of the Civil War, when a band of Union sympathizers, called the Kansas Red Legs, rode onto their Missouri farm and ordered her to make biscuits for all of them. Grandfather Young was away on one of his wagon trips, and so his wife made biscuits while the Red Legs butchered four hundred hogs, hacked out their hams, slung them over their saddles, then rode away, to pillage other farms in the area. Grandmother Young never forgave the Union Army or Abraham Lincoln for what happened. The incident kept her a confirmed Confederate.

The Solomon Youngs and the Anderson Trumans had long been neighbors and friends, and their farms in Jackson County, Missouri, were only three miles apart. Among their many children, the Youngs had a daughter named Martha Ellen, and the Trumans had a son named John. John was a short, quiet boy whose nickname, Peanuts, stayed with him the rest of his life.

When he was still a boy, John told his father that he wanted to be a mule trader when he grew up.

"Well," said his father, trying not to smile, "it is not always regarded as the highest calling in the world, but always tell the truth and nobody will believe you."

At the time, Grandfather Truman, a quiet, gentle man, was the director of Jackson County's thirty-two schools, each of which had only a single teacher. The family lived on a two-hundred-acre farm near Westport Landing, Missouri—which later became Kansas City.

According to the Jackson County record of the time: "John Anderson Truman resides with his father and manages the farm: he is an industrious and energetic young man and one that bids fair to make a success in life."

But success never completely came to John Truman.

Years later, when somebody told Harry that his father must frankly be regarded as a failure, he flashed an angry look and said, "My father was not a failure. After all, he was the father of a President of the United States."

Talking about his father at other times, Truman noted the energy of the man, how he worked regularly from daylight to dark. His father, he said, had raised him on a code of

13

honor and integrity, on the sharp and constant need to put honor above profit. When his father said something about a horse or a cow or a piece of land, everybody knew it was the truth. "He lived what he believed," said Truman, "and taught the rest of us to do the same thing. He was a doer, not a talker."

Small and wiry, with a sense of humor that practically knocked off people's hats when they weren't looking, John Truman had the local reputation for being "the kind of man who never passed a cow but what he stopped and tried to buy her." But at the age of thirty, just before he got married, he was still managing his father's farm.

John Truman and Martha Ellen Young had known each other most of their lives. She was a small, slender girl with dark hair and eyes of mischief, who loved to read and ride, showed a strong talent in music and art, and laughingly described herself as "a lightfooted Baptist" because she adored dancing. She had attended the Baptist College for Women, and she was twenty-nine when she and John Truman were married.

The newlyweds moved to Lamar, Missouri, a quiet and pretty country village, less than a hundred miles from the borders of Kansas, Oklahoma and Arkansas. Like many towns of the time, it was built around a square, with a courthouse in the middle, and all of it shaded with huge elm and maple trees. It was a town of eight hundred people and serviced the farmers in the nearby rolling country who came in regularly to buy their supplies. John Truman bought a small frame house with a porch and a bay window. Here in this small house, near the Blue and the Big Blue rivers

14

and the rugged rambling hills, Harry S. Truman was born on May 8, 1884.

The day his son was born, John Truman nailed a horseshoe on the door of his white cottage, and planted a pine tree. (That pine tree was seventy feet tall when Harry Truman became President.) The name Harry was a shortened version of Harrison, his mother's brother. Uncle Harrison was one of his favorites, a big man, as strong as a wrestler, who lived in nearby Kansas City and always arrived with candy, nuts and lots of good stories.

They added the initial "S" to Harry's name to please relatives on both sides, since one grandfather was named Solomon and the other Shippe. By the time Harry was three years old, he had a baby brother, Vivian; and two years later, a sister, Mary Jane.

In the meantime, the John Truman family had moved back to the Solomon Young farm. Just before Christmas, 1890, they moved to nearby Independence, a small city close to Kansas City that had served as the jumping-off place for both the Santa Fe Trail and the Oregon Trail. The pioneer travelers on both those trails had started to settle the West long before the railroads. Those who stayed to settle in the Great Plains were the hardy ones who faced the quick-changing weather of heat and drought and bitter cold. In nearby western Kansas, in a single year, some thirty thousand newcomers gave up and went back east. On the sides of many of their wagons were signs, "IN GOD WE TRUSTED, IN KANSAS WE BUSTED."

John Truman was one of those who stayed. He bought a house with a large barn and a back lot of several acres not

15

far from the Missouri Pacific Railroad tracks. He fenced in his back lot and filled it with all kinds of animals that he bought and traded.

Harry Truman was six years old then and he remembered one time when his father had five hundred goats in the back lot, but John Truman kept his animal population constantly changing. He also operated another farm southeast of town, bought and sold real estate and actively participated in local Democratic politics. He sometimes participated so actively that he came home bloodied from political fights that had turned into fist fights.

While the shy boy with thick glasses deeply admired his fighting father, his mother kept him quietly corralled.

She started him early on piano-playing, and gave him his first lessons on their old upright. Later he went to a neighborhood teacher, and finally to a well-known piano teacher in nearby Kansas City, Mrs. E. C. White. Mrs. White rapped his knuckles with her pencil when he missed a note, helped fill him with a real love for music, insisting on his practicing two hours every day.

He started school when he was eight. Even before that, his mother sent him to Sunday school. Though he was born and bred a Baptist, the nearest Sunday school was at the First Presbyterian Church, and so he went there.

That's where he met Elizabeth Virginia Wallace, a very beautiful little girl with lovely blue eyes and the prettiest golden curls he had ever seen.

Everybody called her Bess, and it suited her perfectly. She was the first girl he ever met who could whistle through her teeth, bat a ball as far as any boy in the neighborhood and bait her own hook when she went fishing. She was also the best tennis player in town, a beautiful skater and a pretty good fighter.

Harry Truman idolized her from a distance—he was so shy he didn't speak to her for five years.

How can a shy boy with thick glasses win the girl he wants—the most popular and the prettiest girl in town? he asked himself. Not by currying and watering and feeding the horses; not by milking the cows; not by marching the goats every morning and evening two blocks to the big public spring.

The only way was to become a hero.

And how does a boy become a hero?

Harry didn't know, but he could try reading about other heroes.

By the time he was twelve he had read most of the books in the Independence Public Library, including the encyclopedias. Two years before, his mother had given him a gift, his most prized possession, a set of books edited by Charles F. Horne called "Great Men and Famous Women." The four separate volumes were entitled *Soldiers and Sailors, Statesmen and Sages, Workmen and Heroes, Artists and Authors.* He read and reread them.

The volume on *Soldiers and Sailors* meant most to him, with men like George Washington, Stonewall Jackson, Jeb Stuart and, especially, Hannibal and General Robert E. Lee. In reading about their lives, he noted several things: the really great men never thought they were great, the really great ones were unselfish patriots—and the first victory they won was over themselves.

That's when he decided he wanted to be a soldier.

He used to daydream about his heroes while he worked at

Jim Clinton's drugstore. It was easy to daydream while he washed windows, swept sidewalks and dusted about a thousand bottles on all the shelves every day. His salary then was three silver dollars a week.

Then his big chance seemed to come. The United States went to war with Spain over Cuba in 1898.

It marked the end of an era. Before that, Americans thought mostly about their own country and little about the world. Our navy was so small that even the South American country of Chile had a bigger navy.

But as we reached the turn of the century, the American people had settled their own frontier. "Americans must now begin to look outward," wrote naval historian Captain Alfred Thayer Mahan. Other historians echoed him. It was not only our duty to expand our interests into the world, they said, but it was our destiny.

The Cuban people had long struggled for independence against Spain, and the American people had a natural sympathy for their cause. American newspapers outdid each other in exaggerating the Spanish "butchery" during the Cuban revolt. President William McKinley wanted no part of any such conflict. But his Assistant Secretary of the Navy, Theodore Roosevelt, who also wore thick glasses, but was not shy, said, "We will have this war for the freedom of Cuba in spite of the timidity of the commercial interests."

After the unexplained explosion of the United States warship *Maine* anchored in Havana Harbor, the United States declared war and sent a force of seventeen thousand troops. One of the heroes was the Rough Rider with thick glasses— Theodore Roosevelt.

Back in Independence, Missouri, fourteen-year-old Harry

Truman followed the war with mounting excitement, and he was among the town teen-agers who formed the Independence Junior Militia. They drilled with .22-caliber rifles, shot an occasional chicken and roasted it on the banks of the river. While they rehashed the latest accounts of the Rough Riders, they all talked hopefully about a war that might wait for them.

But the war wouldn't wait. Within ten weeks, Spain had surrendered.

If Harry Truman was downcast by the sudden end of the war, he was more determined than ever to become a soldier. He confided this to his favorite high school teacher, Miss Margaret Phelps, who taught history. His ambition, he said, was to go to West Point. Miss Phelps volunteered to give him special coaching at night to prepare him for the West Point examinations. But when the time came, they turned him down—his eyesight was too poor.

It was a strong blow for a boy who wanted to be a soldier, and a hero. Nor was it very consoling thinking back to his books about heroes, that their first victory was the one they had won over themselves!

In a sense, high school student Harry Truman had partly won that victory. In the formation of the Independence Junior Militia, much of his shyness had disappeared. He was still punctual and obedient, and all his teachers remembered him as being a hard worker. If they didn't consider him a brilliant student, the teachers nonetheless found him highly satisfactory.

But he gave up his piano practice. "I decided that it was a sissy thing to be a piano player, and I quit," he said, and then added, "I wasn't good enough." He never gave up his

19

love for music, however, and his favorites were Chopin, Mozart, Bach and Beethoven. In the years to come, his favorite relaxation would be sitting at the piano and playing waltzes or études. And he didn't quit before he composed a piano piece which featured Bess Wallace's private whistle (the one she made through her teeth) as the main theme in the composition.

He and Bess Wallace were high school seniors now and she even let him carry her books home sometimes. She was still the belle, the beauty and the most popular girl in the class, and Harry Truman was just a nice boy, nothing very special.

One of the special things in young Harry's life at that time was the Democratic National Convention in Kansas City in 1900. Mr. Truman, who had become a successful grain speculator, had enough political influence to get his son Harry a job as a convention page.

The Democratic party candidate for President had run unsuccessfully four years before and would run unsuccessfully a third time. But for the seventeen thousand people in that Kansas City hall, including Harry, young William Jennings Bryan, with the flowing hair and the bell-like voice, was their hero.

Bryan lost to President McKinley in that November election mainly because the United States was at a peak of prosperity and McKinley's campaign promised "four more years of the full dinner pail."

The United States in 1900 had seventy-six million citizens, and women won the right to vote in four western states. Women also wore dresses long enough to hide their ankles, and paid fourteen cents a dozen for eggs and four cents a pound for sugar. Throughout the country there were only ten miles of concrete road and some eight thousand automobiles, of which one third were electric, the others operating on steam.

For high school senior Harry Truman, at the turn of the century, the future seemed very uncertain, except that he knew he wanted to continue his education. It was mainly his mother, that tiny, strong-minded woman who impressed upon him his moral code. She filled him with a real sense of duty and responsibility, told him that idleness was a sin, that people had to work for what they got, that people did what they had to do.

It was his mother, too, who shaped his religious education. By the time he was twelve, he had finished reading the family Bible for the second time. For him, religion was a simple, uncomplicated faith, and he believed in prayer without pretense. His directions on how to live with other people came from the twentieth chapter of Exodus and the fifth chapter of Deuteronomy, and his formula for living came from the Sermon on the Mount.

He learned to judge people mostly by what they did rather than by what they said. He noticed that many of the people who talked the loudest about closing the town saloons still came to Jim Clinton's drugstore every morning for their daily "prescription" drink of whiskey.

He was growing up. His closest friend, and the school's most brilliant boy, was Charles Ross, son of the town's jailer. The two boys shared a similar feeling for history and Latin. Together they built a bridge, whittled out of wood, pat-

21

terned exactly on the description in Julius Caesar's "Commentaries" of one of his military bridges across the Rhine River. It took them a month.

"I saw that it takes men to make history," said Truman, "or there would be no history. History does not make the man."

The two boys also put out the high school paper, *The Gleam,* which featured the quotation:

> Over the margin
> After it, follow it,
> Follow the gleam.

It was a motto a young man could aim at: "Follow the gleam."

It tied together well with what his mother taught him. But the gleam seemed a more distant dream for Harry Truman than for Charlie Ross. It was Charlie who gave the high school valedictorian speech on Shakespeare. It was Charlie who won all the scholarship honors. And it was Charlie who was grabbed and kissed and congratulated by one of their favorite teachers, Miss Tillie Brown.

"Harry was standing by," said another teacher, Mrs. Palmer, and he asked, 'Well, don't I get one, too?'

"Miss Brown said, 'Not until you have done something worthwhile!'

"Years later," continued Mrs. Palmer, "when Harry became President of the United States, he selected Charles Ross to be his press secretary, and the first night they were together, Charlie said, 'Wouldn't Miss Tillie be glad to know we are together again?'

"Harry just picked up the phone," said Mrs. Palmer, "and put in a call for Independence and Miss Brown and said, 'Hello, Miss Brown, this is the President of the United States, do I get that kiss?' "

"Yes, come and get it," she said.

It was Miss Tillie Brown who remembered how Harry always squared his shoulders before speaking.

Now, as he was graduated from high school (he was one of eleven boys in a graduating class of forty-one), he squared his shoulders at a still uncertain future. In his wallet he had a copy of a poem by Alfred Lord Tennyson called "Locksley Hall." It was a poem he would carry in his wallet for the rest of his life, and it began:

For I dipt into the future, far as human eye can see,
Saw the vision of the world and all the wonder that would
  be. . . .

☆ ☆ ☆ ☆ ☆ **2**

ONE OF THE HIGHLY PUBLICIZED NEWS STORIES in 1901, when slim, serious Harry Truman was graduated from high school, was the day-by-day account of a Chicago schoolboy sent on a trip around the world by a Chicago newspaper. He made the record-breaking trip in sixty days, thirteen hours, twenty-nine minutes and forty-two and four-fifths seconds.

How Harry Truman envied that boy!

His own future seemed so bleak. He had hoped to go to college but his father's speculation in wheat had suddenly turned bad, and the family found itself deep in debt. The immediate need was for quick cash.

Harry took the first available job, that of timekeeper, for thirty-five dollars a month, with meals. The company he worked for operated three camps for four hundred men to improve a long stretch of the Santa Fe Railroad tracks. It meant living in tents, eating out of tin pans, learning to talk the language of rough men. He later said he learned "all the cuss words of the English language—not by ear but by note."

Many of these men were hoboes, who had traveled to different corners of the country, and Harry listened with

25

wonder to the stories they told. They were not the stories you find in history books, but stories that burned deep into a young man's mind, stories of the birth and death of mining towns in the wild West, the new booming oil towns in Texas started by a gusher that shot two hundred feet in the air, stories that told what it was really like during that land rush in Oklahoma when they opened up the Indian territory to all settlers.

Among other things, that job also gave Harry a special feeling for trains, and that knowledge and that feeling later played an important part in his life when he was a United States Senator.

That job lasted almost nine months. When he came home again, no longer a boy, he found the family's financial situation even worse. His father had a small, single hope left—some forty acres of land he still owned in southern Missouri. Hiring a buggy and a horse, father and son drove down to get their first look at this land, to see if it was a place where the family might make a fresh start, or whether it was even salable. They drove along the Eleven Point River, which was then flooded. The water came up to the bottom of the buggy each time they crossed the river, and they crossed it thirteen times in eight miles. When they finally found their land, they saw how unusable it was—it ran straight up the side of a mountain!

Back home, Harry took a job wrapping newspapers in the mailing room of the Kansas City *Star*—for seven dollars a week. His father was forced to sell their home and buy a smaller one. At fifty-one, he seemed a broken man. The city directory which had listed John Truman as a livestock dealer, soon listed him as a watchman—night watchman at the Missouri Elevator Company in Kansas City.

On September 6, 1901, President McKinley was assassinated, and Rough Rider Roosevelt became the new President of the United States. Queen Victoria of England had died earlier that year, changing the course of that country, and Kaiser Wilhelm of Germany had started building a strong army for a future war. That war would change Harry Truman's life, but he didn't know it then.

All he knew now was that his family desperately needed more money. His sister was still at school but his brother Vivian worked in the National Bank of Commerce in Kansas City, and Harry also took a job there. They put him in that part of the bank they called "the zoo." It was a caged section in the basement where Harry handled all the checks that came in from some twelve hundred other banks in the area. His job was to mark down the amount and source of each check. For him, it was boring work, but it paid thirty-five dollars a month.

His father tried his hand at many things, but his luck stayed bad. He had traded his house for eighty acres of land, worked hard to produce a big corn crop, but then a sudden flood washed it all away.

By the time he was twenty, Harry had another job as bookkeeper, this time at the Union Central Bank, for sixty dollars a month. Living was cheap then. He and his brother Vivian paid five dollars a week for room and board, which included breakfast and dinner. A box lunch cost ten cents and they could go to a movie for a nickel.

On Saturday afternoons Harry worked as an usher at the local vaudeville house and saw all the shows for nothing.

He saved most of his salary and sent it home to his family. One of his fellow boarders, Arthur Eisenhower (whose brother Dwight would succeed Truman as President) re-

membered those early days and said, "Harry and I had only
a dollar a week left over for riotous living."

Harry helped make his own fun at the boardinghouse,
playing the piano, creating a community sing. On weekends
he headed home to the family farm for his mother's fried
chicken, hot biscuits and custard pie.

He had begun to enjoy his life in Kansas City, and his
bank salary had doubled in the past two years, but once
again his life changed. His father told him he planned to
give up his farm and move to Grandma Young's farm near
Grandview, but it was too large a farm to manage by himself, and he needed his two sons.

It meant a change from the soft city life to the hard farm
life, and Harry Truman didn't want to be a farmer. While
he liked the feel of a farmer's life, the closeness to growing
things, the simplicity, the peace, he saw no personal future
in it. He preferred the exhilarating contact of city life, the
many friends, the concerts, the vaudeville, the fun. Farming
meant work from dawn to dark—and loneliness. But what
could he say to his father who needed him? So, without
question, Harry quit his bank job and brought his soft city
hands back to the rough work of the farm. Vivian came too,
but soon returned to the city, and many of Harry's Kansas
City friends made bets that he, too, would soon return.

But he stayed. He stayed almost a dozen years.

His mother always said that Harry got his common sense
on the farm, not in town. She was also the one who insisted
that Harry could plant the straightest row of corn in the
whole county.

It wasn't easy. Their horses were lively and sometimes had
their own ideas about where they wanted to go. The plan

28

was to adjust the corn planter before starting, then keep the horses well in hand and under control, pick out an object on the other side of the field, usually a quarter of a mile away, point the tongue of the planter at that object and keep it there, then let the horses step out at a lively gait, fast and straight ahead.

His father kept a critical eye on things, and if a blank space or a crooked row showed up in the cornfield, he would not let Harry forget it.

His father also taught him how to make clean fence corners, control weeds and operate a gang plow. A gang plow had two twelve-inch plows on the same frame, with three wheels, all pulled by four horses or mules. Harry learned the difficult trick of forcing these four horses to come around sharply at the end of a furrow, making a neat left turn to start out straight again on the next furrow.

He had persuaded his father to try new methods of soil conservation and crop rotation and labor-saving machinery. He had the personal satisfaction of starting a county farm bureau to help farmers with their problems. The first farm club for young people in western Missouri was organized by him.

But it was a lonely life, riding a gang plow all day long, with nobody to talk to but the four horses. His own horizons seemed so small. Was the boundary of this farm going to be the shape of his world? He saw himself as a small farmer in a small town with a small-sized future. His dream girl Bess Wallace was still mostly a dream. She had gone to the Barstow School for Girls and starred on its basketball team; she had her own beautiful black horse and two greyhounds; and she even knew how to drive her father's Studebaker.

The only time he saw her was when he returned a cake plate to her mother from his aunt in Independence. But he knew that the Wallace family hardly regarded him as a proper suitor for their highly popular Bess. After all, Harry Truman had neither money nor a future, and he could readily understand that they wouldn't want their Bess married to an ordinary farmer.

And that's just what he seemed to be then, an ordinary farmer.

His main social life came from the Masonic Lodge which he had joined, just as his grandfathers had long before. He helped organize the Grandview Lodge and soon became one of its high officers.

Another sidelight of interest at the time was his first political job. His father had been made one of the thirty-six road overseers in Jackson County, and also served as an elections judge. Harry became his clerk.

But that was scarcely enough for a restless young man, when the outside world was stirring and shaking. Harry kept up with the living history of the newspapers. He had seen President Roosevelt pull the United States deeper into world affairs, even help settle a war between Russia and Japan and a crisis in Morocco in 1905; he had seen the start of the Panama Canal, the quick growth of our Navy. He had seen President Roosevelt hand-pick his presidential successor, William Howard Taft, in 1908, then fight him four years later in a bitter battle at the Republican National Convention. When Taft won, Roosevelt started his own Progressive party and Woodrow Wilson was narrowly elected President in a close three-cornered race.

Politics excited Harry, just as it had excited his father, but there was something now that excited him even more. The map of Europe had split up into armed camps, and Kaiser Wilhelm II felt that his Germany was then strong enough to rule the Continent.

War was brewing in the Balkans and a typical newspaper headline read: "GREAT EUROPEAN WAR LOOMS ON HORIZON." There were also revolutions in nearby Mexico, and increasing newspaper talk that we might be forced to send an expeditionary force to quiet it.

Here was Harry's chance to dust off his dream of becoming a soldier. Together with other young men in town, he became a charter member of Battery B of the Missouri National Guard. The sixty men of Battery B met once a week at the armory and paid a quarter a week dues for the privilege of drilling.

When Battery B trained outdoors, they rented horses from a local moving firm. Private Truman not only learned how to handle these horses in army maneuvers, but he learned some fencing, ju-jitsu and served as Number Two man on the three-inch gun. Nobody cared then that Harry Truman wore thick glasses—the only thing that mattered was his willingness to drill and learn.

But Grandmother Young did care about something else. She had not forgotten the blue-uniformed Union soldiers who had raided her farm during the Civil War. The first time Harry appeared in his grandmother's house wearing the blue uniform of the National Guard, she blasted him. "Harry! This is the first time a uniform of that color has been in this house since the Civil War. Don't bring it back!"

He was proud of his uniform which he never wore to his grandmother's house. And he was proud of being a sol-

31

dier, even if only part-time. However, he was still a full-time farmer, up at four-thirty on a summer morning to start the binder before sunrise. The work seldom eased: plowing, sowing, reaping, baling hay, feeding and doctoring the animals, even helping his mother with the meals.

His one extravagance was a secondhand four-cylinder Stafford automobile that had a high brass windshield and Prest-O-Lite lamps.

For Harry Truman, the most important thing about his six-hundred-dollar automobile was that it made it a lot easier to court Bess Wallace. He had made up his mind, farmer or no farmer, he was in love with Bess. He traveled the twenty miles from Grandview to Independence by horseback or buggy, or sometimes by train. Then Bess's father died, and she and her mother moved in with her grandmother. The Wallace family had never thought much of Harry as a suitor, but now that he had a car, they all seemed to pay a bit more attention to him. When he called to take Bess on a picnic, sometimes her two brothers and their girl friends went along for the ride.

Harry was thirty years old in 1914 when his father died.

He seemed caught. He could hardly go away and leave his mother and sister to run the farm. And he still didn't want to be a farmer, since the Wallace family seemed more determined than ever not to have Bess become a farmer's wife.

What could he do? Some friends told him about a promising zinc mine at Commerce, Oklahoma, one hundred and fifty miles away and persuaded him to become a working partner and get rich. Every weekend he helped work the mine, but instead of getting rich, each of the partners came out losing seventy-five hundred dollars.

In the meantime, the county politicians gave Harry his father's old job of road overseer. In those days, the road overseer not only bossed repair crews on the roads, but also collected taxes. Harry took his job so seriously that he proposed plans for a complete road overhaul in the area. Officials decided that the Truman plan was too ambitious and so they appointed somebody else to the job. But they did give him a political appointment as Grandview postmaster—a job he kept while he continued to work the farm.

He was still a part-time soldier but his chances of becoming a hero were pretty remote. President Wilson did send troops into Mexico but he had no need of the Missouri National Guard.

However, a war in Europe had started. The Archduke of Austria-Hungary had been assassinated on June 28, 1914, and all Europe was soon split into sides in a total war. President Wilson, however, quickly announced America's neutrality. We would take no sides, he said.

Just as his father had speculated in wheat, Harry Truman began speculating in oil. He became a one-third partner in the Morgan Oil and Refining Company. Because of his bookkeeping experience at the bank, he acted as treasurer.

In an appeal for stockholders, the company noted in its newspaper ad:

In the event this country is unfortunately brought to war, the absolute necessity of gasoline and other by-products of crude petroleum are bound to come to such an urgent demand that the price will soar beyond all expectations, and an investment in the shares of any oil company that has production and large holdings of proven properties, with its thousands of acres of probable oil producing territory, with its own refinery for the refining of the crude product ready for the market, such as held and owned by Morgan Oil and Refining Company, is beyond question an investment of rare opportunity.

The ad was right, absolutely right, but its timing was wrong. It was true that the company controlled some twenty thousand acres in Kansas, more acres in Texas and added acres in Oklahoma. But so far, the company had not hit any oil. On one of its properties in Eureka, Kansas, the northwestern corner of Greenwood County, the company had dug a test oil well some nine hundred feet down, then gave up. If they had persisted in digging deeper, just another nine hundred feet, they would have hit the largest oil area in the state of Kansas. Another company took over their leases, continued drilling and found that famous oil area now known as the Teeter Pool. It was an oil pool that made many many millionaires.

Thirty years later, Harry Truman discussed the oil well business in a letter to his former partner, David Morgan, and wrote:

"Maybe I wouldn't be Pres if we'd hit."

It was true. That oil well might have made him a millionaire, but it was World War I that helped make him President of the United States.

☆　　☆　　☆　　☆　　☆　　**3**

PRESIDENT MCKINLEY HADN'T WANTED WAR
with Spain in 1898, and President Wilson didn't want war
with Germany in 1917, but in each case public pressure for
war mounted like a fever. And in both cases newspapers
fanned the fever, while the sinking of our ships raised the
intensity of American anger to the exploding point. In 1898,
there was the unexplained sinking of the *Maine,* and in
1915 there was the German sinking of the *Lusitania,* with
the loss of 1,446 lives.

President Wilson was re-elected in 1916, on the campaign
slogan, "He kept us out of war," but the American public
mood had changed from neutrality to armed neutrality.
Our friendly favoring of the Allies against the Germans
grew constantly stronger. As the Germans sank more of
our ships, the United States finally declared war on April 6,
1917.

When war came, Harry Truman's old Battery B suddenly expanded into six batteries of field artillery. Private
Truman had been promoted to corporal and hoped to be
made a section sergeant. At that time, though, enlisted men
elected their own officers, and the boys of Battery B elected
Truman First Lieutenant.

The onetime shyness of the small boy with thick glasses had completely disappeared. Not only was he the most popular man in Battery B, but he was the one picked to recruit volunteers for the battery. He now had an open-top red roadster, a winning smile, a firm handshake. The loneliness of the farmer gave way to the strong self-confidence of the soldier.

He was thirty-three and now it was Bess Wallace who wanted to marry him, and it was Harry who said no. There was a war on. He could be crippled; he might be killed—and where would that leave her? No, they had best wait till the war was over.

He had dreamed the dream so long and now it suddenly seemed as if everything was going to come true. He had won the heart of the girl he loved, he had become a soldier, popular among his men, and there was the chance that he might even become a hero!

But Truman's first Army assignment was hardly an exciting one. He was put in charge of Battery F, and they were all sent for further training at Fort Sill, Oklahoma, where he was given the added job of regimental canteen officer. This meant that he was supposed to set up a store and service facilities for the soldiers in the regiment. For his assistant, Truman picked Sergeant Edward Jacobson, who later became his good friend and business partner.

Truman and Jacobson collected two dollars from each man in the outfit. It added up to twenty-two hundred dollars. They then set up a store and filled it with everything soldiers might want, from cigarettes to sweaters. They also opened a barber shop and a tailor shop. Most of the other canteens at Fort Sill lost money but the Truman-Jacobson canteen showed a fifteen-thousand-dollar profit after six months. That profit was divided among all the soldiers in the regiment.

This seemingly unimportant canteen job helped change Truman's army career, as well as the future course of his life.

Because of his success with this canteen, he was picked as one of ten officers sent to France for advanced training, ahead of the regiment. Because of that advanced training, Truman found himself promoted to captain and commanding officer of Battery D of the One hundred and twenty-ninth Field Artillery of the Thirty-fifth Division.

Before the promotion came through, the commanding officer checked Truman's efficiency rating and returned it with the comment, "No man can be that good." In a heated moment, that same officer yelled at Truman, "It will be a disaster to the country to let you command men!"

But he was wrong on both counts. When a boy dreams a single dream hard enough and long enough, until it becomes part of his blood and bone, it cannot be wiped away by another man's sneer.

But the challenge was sharp. Before Truman took it over, Battery D was better known as "the dizzy D." The men in it were known as "the Fighting Irish," and they were rough and rowdy. None of their three previous commanding officers had lasted very long. One of them had even suffered a nervous breakdown. They privately mocked at this mild-looking man in glasses, and greeted his arrival by staging a small riot. Besides breaking cots and chairs, and sending four men to the army hospital, they also started a fake stampede of some of their horses.

But the soft city bank clerk had been toughened by the farm, and he still remembered his summer training alongside the tough railroad workers when he was seventeen.

Truman was scared that first day with Battery D, but none of that fear showed in his face or voice or decisions. He called in his noncommissioned officers, sternly told them that they would be completely responsible for keeping discipline among their men, and he assured them that if they couldn't do it, he would get other noncoms who could. "I didn't come here to get along with you," Truman told them. "You've got to get along with me." If they couldn't, he wanted them to speak up—and he would bust them back to private right then and there.

Nobody spoke.

That did it. Truman and his troops got along so well afterward that Battery D soon lost much of its "dizzy" reputation and picked up a new efficiency. Under Captain Truman, the 188 men of the battery learned to prepare four guns for movement and combat, together with their wagons, ammunition, horses, carriages and field kitchens —all ready to go anywhere within fourteen minutes.

Truman earned not only the respect of his men; he also earned their affection. He marched and slept in the same mud they did, often without a pup tent; when a big gun got stuck, his shoulders were usually among those trying to push or pull it; and whenever possible, Captain Truman gave his men permission to leave camp, lent them money when they needed it, even joined them in their poker games.

Talking about it long afterward, Truman said, "I always tried to do every job I got better than anybody had ever done it before."

Something else he had learned long before, from his study of history, was that a leader is a man who has the ability to get other people to do what they don't want to do—and like it.

The test came when his outfit was ordered to the front lines. It was supposedly a quiet sector high on Mount Herrenberg in the picturesque Vosges Mountains of eastern France. Orders came for Battery D' to fire its first barrage, some five hundred gas shells. The Germans quickly and accurately retaliated.

Two of the Battery guns were stuck in the mud and the men were trying to get them out when the German shells started falling all around them, and close. "Run, boys," yelled a sergeant, "they've got a bracket on us." Except for five men, the whole Battery panicked and ran into the nearby forest.

One of the five who stayed behind was Captain Truman. His horse had slipped in a shell hole, throwing him and rolling over on him. By the time he got up, the men had scattered.

"I got up and called them everything I knew," said Truman. "Pretty soon, they came sneaking back."

Ashamed of themselves, and impressed by the courage of their captain, the boys of Battery D redeemed themselves many times before the war was over. They even learned to laugh at themselves for that incident, referring to it mockingly as "The Battle of Who Run."

Instead of court-martialing the panicky sergeant, as the

colonel requested, Captain Truman had him busted to a lower rank and transferred to another outfit. "I didn't care for court-martial," said Truman. "I'd get myself back of a table and I'd look as mean as I could. Then I'd tell them, 'You can have a court-martial or, if you prefer, you can take what I give you.'"

They not only took what he gave them, but they respected him all the more for it. The morale of Battery D zoomed.

It zoomed even higher just before one of the big battles of the war, the critical Meuse-Argonne offensive. One of his fellow officers, Edward Condon, remembered a short talk Truman gave his men just before the battle: "I want to tell you fellows," said Truman, "right tonight, I'm where I want to be—in command of this battery. I'd rather be right here than President of the United States. You boys are my kind! Now let's go!"

In that Meuse-Argonne offensive, more than a million American soldiers in twenty-seven Army divisions had the job of smashing the final German defense of the Hindenburg Line.

Early in the morning of the offensive, the four seventy-five millimeter guns of Battery D fired three thousand rounds of ammunition within the first four hours.

"I had slept in the edge of the wood to the right of my battery position," said Truman. "If I hadn't awakened and got up at 4:00 A.M., I would not be here, because the Germans fired a barrage on my sleeping place!"

Captain Truman often went on personal reconnaissance to observe enemy fire so that he could direct counterfire from his own battery onto the enemy positions. "I was up in front of the infantry without a weapon of any kind," said Truman, "observing the enemy fire from every direction. An infantry sergeant came up to my foxhole and told me that my support had moved back two hundred yards, and that I'd do well to come back too. I did!"

On another personal reconnaissance, Truman found himself pinned down by German machine gun fire for several hours. His men had almost given him up for lost when he finally reappeared, and showed them his new path past the barbed wire.

During still another reconnaissance, Captain Truman spied a large-sized force of German troops moving toward the side of his frontline division position. At that time the Captain was under strict orders to fire only at German positions directly in front of him. This new movement of Germans was just outside his ordered area of fire. The Germans were moving so fast, Captain Truman knew there was no time to contact headquarters and outline the situation. If he did, it would be too late to stop the German movement. If he disobeyed orders, he could be court-martialed; if he disregarded his own judgment, it might cost the lives of many American soldiers.

Truman acted quickly, instinctively. He directed his four guns to fire at the German force. The Battery D barrage knocked out two enemy batteries and an observation post, helped take most of the steam out of the German surprise attack and saved the day on the American Thirty-fifth Division front. For what he did, Truman was neither praised nor court-martialed. "All I received," wrote Truman in a memo later, "was a scolding for shooting out of the division sector!"

Throughout the dirt and smoke of battle, Captain Truman amazed his men, not only by his coolness, but also by his neatness, his clean-shaven look. Lieutenant Harry Vaughan visited him one day from a neighboring battery, and commented afterward, "Dirt and cooties didn't seem to stick to him the way they did to the rest of us . . . he must have shaved with coffee because we didn't have plain hot water."

Vaughan became a close friend and political supporter of Truman, and went to the White House with him as a military aide.

Another Truman friend and fellow officer was James M. Pendergast, whose father and Uncle Tom were political bosses whose influence stretched all over the state of Missouri.

Still another fellow officer, whose political life was to cross Truman's in many important ways, was Lieutenant Colonel Bennett Clark, son of Champ Clark, noted Speaker of the House of Representatives. Truman's first contact with Clark was in a frontline sector where his battery had recently arrived for further orders. Truman saw that Colonel Clark's headquarters area was littered with dead horses, and Clark quickly explained. "The enemy has been blasting this place every hour on the hour. Here are your orders and maps . . . better get out of here . . . I don't want you to suffer the fate of those poor horses."

Within twenty minutes, Truman had his equipment ready, his horses hitched, his guns rolling out of the area, hunting for cover. Hours later the area was still completely quiet, and Truman checked in again with Colonel Clark. The Colonel stood there laughing. It was all a big joke. "The Germans haven't fired here at all," said Clark. As for the dead horses, he explained that a veterinarian had ordered them shot because they had an infectious disease which could not be cured but could infect the other healthy horses. Truman joined in the laughter.

Victory was now near and one day the men of Battery D happily circulated a French newspaper which reported that the Armistice had been signed. While the men celebrated, some big German shells landed nearby. "Captain," said one of the sergeants, "those——Germans haven't seen this paper."

The war had taken many turns since its start in 1914. The Germans had swept into France through Belgium, but then the French forces, helped by a small British Army, stopped the Germans in the Battle of the Marne. The Germans, however, still had superior strength in men and equipment, and tried to seize all the ports and cut off supplies coming from England. This time the British troops held them back, and then the war changed into trench warfare, both sides digging in behind barbed wire. It was a war of poison gas, big guns, and the tank was still something new in war, as were the zepplin and the airplane. Italy fought against Germany then, and Russia also fought on the side of the Allies. But in 1917 there was a revolution in Russia, the Czar was overthrown, and a Soviet government took over and made a separate peace with Germany. This released more German soldiers to fight against the Allies. At this crucial point, the Americans came into the war. The fresh force of American troops and supplies helped turn the tide. Before it was all over, however, more than four years of war had killed more than ten million people.

The Armistice was finally signed on November 11, 1918,

and Truman remembered that it was so quiet, it made his head ache. That night, though, there was noise enough for everybody, but of a different kind. French soldiers visited Battery D, bringing many bottles of wine, and yelling, *"Vive President Wilson, Vive Le Capitaine D'Artillerie Americaine!"* So many flares filled the sky that night that it looked like the Fourth of July.

That night Captain Harry Truman must have felt an enormous sense of satisfaction. The war was over, he was still alive—and that meant he could go home and marry the woman he loved. In addition, he had fought through this war and had proved his courage and leadership. If he was not a hero in the dramatic sense that Rough Rider Theodore Roosevelt had been a hero in the Spanish-American War, still, Captain Harry Truman proved himself a hero to his men. Battery D pooled their money and bought him a huge silver loving cup.

While Harry Truman received no special citations for his bravery and judgment, the regimental historian wrote this:

How many men of the infantry, digging in on the open hillsides, overhanging Charpentry and Beulny, owe their lives to the alertness, initiative and efficiency of Captain Truman and to the quick responsiveness and trained efficiency of his men at the guns.

But if this scene was over, the play had still just begun, and the characters were the same. Pendergast, Vaughan, Clark, the men of his battery and his regiment, would all form the hard core of a new career for Harry Truman.

One of the most famous songs of World War I was called, "How you gonna keep them down on the Farm after they've seen Paree."

But seeing Paris had nothing to do with Harry Truman's firm decision not to return to the family farm. He had made up his mind a long time ago that farming was not for him. He wanted more out of life than he could get from a farm, more of the daily excitement of living. Besides, no matter how hard he had worked, the family farm never seemed to catch up on its debts, always seemed to owe money to the bank.

Now the war had helped him make the break with the farm. The Army discharged him on May 6, 1919, with the rank of major. Two days later, he celebrated his thirty-fifth birthday.

Yet he saw himself at a crossroads, a man without direction, without even a dream any more. His service in the Army had convinced him that he no longer wanted to spend his life as a soldier.

But what else did he want to do, what else *could* he do?

He just didn't know. He had never been trained for anything but farming and clerking. Fortunately, he had some money and eighty acres of land which he had inherited from his Uncle Harrison. And he still had Bess Wallace waiting for him.

Just before he went overseas, when he was on a train heading for the embarkation port of New York, the train stopped for a short while in Rosedale, Kansas. Truman asked the train switchman if he had enough time to call his girl back home. "Call her," said the switchman. "But if you call her at four o'clock in the morning and she doesn't break the engagement, she really loves you."

She really didn't mind being wakened at that hour; she really did love him. And so, six weeks after his Army discharge, Harry Truman and Bess Wallace were married on June 28, 1919, in the Trinity Episcopal Church in Independence.

The Independence *Examiner* described the ceremony as "a wedding of unusual beauty and interest." The beauty came from the bride, and from some tall cathedral candles that lit up the small, red brick building. The unusual interest came from the age of the couple—both thirty-five—and from the fact that they had shared their childhood and youth and had been willing to wait.

After a short honeymoon trip to Chicago and Detroit, Mr. and Mrs. Harry Truman moved into the elegant, high-ceilinged, fourteen-room Wallace home. Mrs. Wallace lived with them.

Meanwhile, Harry's mother and sister returned to their farm. At the death of the Solomon Youngs, the farm had been divided among Martha Ellen and her three children. Harry took his claim in cash, and so Vivian and Mary Jane divided his share. While Harry was away in the war, Mary Jane had become an expert in farm management, with a good crew of hired hands to help. Harry and Bess often came to visit and he and Mary Jane played classical duets on the old upright piano. On many of those occasions Vivian would also join them.

During his previous business ventures into mining and oil speculation, Harry's family took mortgages on their land to help supply him with whatever money he needed. Now they assured him they would do it again if he wanted to get started on something.

But what was Harry going to do?

It all happened accidentally. He met his old army buddy, Eddie Jacobson in Kansas City. The two men reminisced about how successful they had been in making a profit on their army canteen.

"Maybe we ought to go into business together," said Harry, "and have a partnership again."

The more they talked, the more exciting it sounded. Why not start a men's furnishings store? The men coming home from the war needed everything, and they had the money to spend. They would have a head start on customers, too, since all the boys in their outfit would certainly head for their store first. Harry would know how to handle the bookkeeping and Eddie could take care of the buying and both could serve as salesmen.

They found a desirable location in the front of the Muehlebach Hotel in downtown Kansas City on Twelfth Street. They raised enough money for thirty-five thousand dollars' worth of inventory and on November 29, 1919, opened for business as:

TRUMAN AND JACOBSON,
MEN'S OUTFITTERS

It was an immediate success. Their old army buddies did come to buy, and so did everybody else. Everybody seemed to have money to spend, and their fifteen-dollar silk shirt was a big seller.

They worked hard. "We opened the store at eight in the morning and closed at nine at night," Jacobson said. They worked six days a week, sold more than seventy thousand dollars' worth of merchandise that first year, with a fair share of profit.

It looked as if Harry Truman had finally found himself.

Then the bubble burst. The price of wheat dropped drastically, and they lost their farmer customers. As for the boys of Battery D, "instead of buying," said Jacobson, "they came in for loans."

The country was in a time of turmoil. The United States had refused to join the League of Nations, and the song "Over There" changed into a new American mood: Over Here. According to the Carnegie Endowment for International Peace, the cash cost of World War I was $337,-946,179,657. The American people wanted to forget the war, and its cost in lives—twice as many people killed than in all the wars of the nineteenth century since Napolean. The new President in 1920 was Warren Harding, elected on a campaign promise of a "return to normalcy."

But "normalcy" refused to come. The people passed the Eighteenth Amendment to the Constitution, prohibiting the sale of liquor, and although it closed up saloons, it opened speakeasies and the era of gangsters. New hate groups sprouted everywhere, particularly the Ku Klux Klan, who wore white sheets and masks and paraded under the slogan of 100 per cent Americanism, while they beat up or bloodied or killed anybody they didn't like, particularly immigrants, Negroes, Jews, Catholics and other minorities.

Prices for everything began to soar, zooming the cost of living, and millions of workers went on strike for higher wages. More and more people found themselves without work because too many businesses collapsed after having tried to expand too quickly. In 1921 more than twenty thousand business firms failed.

"Truman and Jacobson, Men's Outfitters," was similarly in trouble. Truman had put up his farm as security for one bank loan in an attempt to satisfy creditors. Their inventory, originally valued at thirty-five thousand dollars was soon worth only ten thousand. The two men made more bank loans, hoping the tide would turn. Instead the value of their inventory kept going down, and they suddenly had to face the fact that they were broke.

Truman's lawyer advised him to declare bankruptcy in 1922. This was perfectly legal and many business firms were doing it. It simply meant that a man admitted legally that he had no more money, and this meant that he was then freed of all debts.

But Harry Truman had been brought up by a family with a different code. They paid what they owed, no matter how long it took, and so would he. It took him fifteen years to pay back all his debts. In the meantime the future looked bleak and bare. The bank had taken over his farm as security, he was heavily in debt and he had lost some thirty thousand dollars.

At thirty-eight he felt he was a failure, a man without a future. He had no money and little hope. Where could he go, what could he do?

☆   ☆   ☆   ☆   ☆

4

THE TINY TOWN OF WESTPORT LANDING OF
Harry Truman's grandfather's day had grown into booming Kansas City, one of the main centers for the country's
cattle and corn. Or as somebody put it, "Here stands a city
built o' bread and beef." Indians covered with blankets still
walked the streets of that city in 1870 when it had a population of thirty-two thousand. By 1880 it had become a
frontier town full of gamblers, with almost as many saloons
as there were grocery stores.

One of the saloonkeepers then was Jim Pendergast, who
soon became the city's most important political boss. There
were many such bosses in the big cities of the United States,
but mainly in those cities where the good citizens themselves refused to be bothered by politics, refused to vote
and organize and campaign for their own candidates. They
were perfectly willing to let somebody else govern their
cities, and so these political bosses became a power. Some
were more honest than others, but most of them operated
on graft and corruption, with many of them becoming
powerful enough to decide which man would be Mayor or
Governor or United States Senator.

Jim Pendergast became that powerful in Missouri. He

called in his three brothers to help him: Tom, John and Mike. It was Mike's son Jim who served as a fellow officer with Harry Truman during the war. It was also young Jim Pendergast who was one of Truman's steady customers at his haberdashery store.

Most important of all, it was Jim Pendergast who told his father what a fine soldier Harry Truman had been, and what a wonderful political candidate he would make.

The elder Jim Pendergast was dead then, and brother Tom Pendergast had taken over. He was a big, burly man, who always wore a derby hat to cover his bald head. Mike, young Jim's father, controlled the Tenth Ward, which had been known as "the old bloody Tenth," because of all the fights there. This area included Jackson County, where Harry Truman lived.

Eastern Jackson County had a Democratic primary scheduled in 1922 to select a candidate for county judge. Missouri county judges were quite different from judges elsewhere. The only judicial decision they made was whether or not a person was insane, and they decided this only with the advice of doctors. Otherwise, Missouri county judges were mostly concerned with local taxes, local roads and county institutions for the poor, the old and the insane.

Harry Truman was in his haberdashery store, just before he went broke. A friend offered him a job with an insurance and loan company, but he couldn't decide whether or not to take it.

Mike Pendergast walked in and soon came to the point. "How'd you like to be county judge?"

Truman hesitated, then asked for time to think it over. He talked it over with a friend of his, Colonel William

Southern, editor of the Independence *Examiner*. Southern tried to discourage him from taking it. He said he knew that Harry was upset by his business failure, but that it was no disgrace to fail in business, that many good men had failed, and had tried again and become successful.

Southern urged him to stay out of politics, warned him that it would mess up his life, told him all the bad effects that constant campaigning could have on the man and on his family. He also told him how poor were the promises and rewards of politics, how unsatisfactory it was to seek the public approval in a never-ending series of elections.

But Truman was not convinced. After thinking it over, he decided the unknown and difficult career of politics was still better than working for a loan company. Besides, it opened a door in a different direction, and he had reached the time of his life when he deeply felt he needed a fresh, new direction.

He told his army buddy, Edgar Hinde, the new postmaster at Independence, what he planned to do.

"I think you're crazy," Hinde told him.

"It might be," said Truman, "but I have to eat."

Hinde said that in that case he would do what he could to help Truman win.

The Independence *Examiner* already had run an earlier item, buried in the bottom of a news column on potential candidates, saying, "Among the younger men, Harry Truman is talked of. Mr. Truman was born and reared in Jackson County and lived for years near Grandview, and his vote in Washington township would be mighty near unanimous if he should run. . . ."

On May 26, under the heading, POLITICAL AN-

NOUNCEMENTS, the Independence *Examiner* ran an ad saying:

We are authorized to announce HARRY S. TRUMAN as a candidate for the Democratic nomination for Judge of the County Court Eastern District. Primary August 1.

Soon afterward Mike Pendergast called a meeting of the Tenth Ward Democratic Club. Each of the seven townships in the county sent representatives, and Truman also came.

"Now I'm going to tell you who you're going to support for county judge," Mike Pendergast told the assembled group. At this point, one man in the group stood up and started accepting congratulations from everybody, but his face changed to a look of surprise and then disappointment when Pendergast said, "It's Harry Truman!"

Mike Pendergast continued: "Harry Truman is a returned soldier, a captain 'over there' with a fine record, whose men didn't want to shoot him!"

Everybody at the meeting assumed that Mike had cleared the Truman nomination with his brother Tom. Later reports rumored that Tom Pendergast had been reluctant about Truman's selection, and had afterward described Truman as "that fellow who went broke with Eddie Jacobson." But everybody also knew that Tom Pendergast usually left Tenth Ward decisions to his brother Mike, because he had enough to keep him busy in Kansas City. Besides, as Truman himself later noted, "Tom never liked the country."

Pendergast approval, however important, didn't guarantee the nomination for Truman. There were four other candidates, including a highly respected banker put up by the rival group.

For Harry Truman, this was much more than a political election. If he failed in this, it would mean, not only the end of a political career that had never started, but it would be another door slamming in his face. He could not fail in this.

County roads were rough in those days, so rough that Truman kept two bags of cement in the back of his Dodge roadster to weight it down so that he would not be thrown through the windshield every time he passed over another bump or another hole.

This was the time when all his old army buddies, all his friends in the National Guard and the Thirty-fifth Division, all the former soldiers who had come to buy at his haberdashery store, now came to help him in his campaign. Some three hundred came from all over Jackson County to a picnic at Lee's Summit, the official opening of his campaign. For entertainment, there was a wrestling match between two brothers, aged eight and nine; an exhibition match by the undefeated amateur welterweight champion of the world; a comedy sketch; a buck and wing dance; and a woman singing "Mother Machree" and "When Irish Eyes Are Smiling."

Then came the candidate, Harry Truman, making his first political speech in front of a public audience.

It was a short speech, and not a very good one. He was scared and rattled and he could hardly be heard. It would take him time to learn how to stir people, how to hit hard with short phrases, how to punctuate his thoughts with proper gesture, how to sell himself.

He soon learned something important: his speeches were much more effective when he honestly felt angry about something.

Something that made him angry now was the fact that somebody discovered that he had once voted for a Republican. Voting for a Republican is probably the deadliest sin of which a Democratic candidate can be accused. Truman could have sidestepped the issue, simply ignoring the charge, never answering it. But this was not a Truman trait. Speaking at a large Democratic campaign rally, the Truman anger caught fire.

He admitted the charge. Yes, he had voted for a Republican. But he had been closer to this man than to a brother. He had fought with him during the war in places "that made hell look like a playground." He had seen this man stick to his post while others were falling back, seen him holding the American line when only three batteries were between the Germans and a successful counterattack. He was proud of this man, proud of his courage, proud of his friendship. He would vote for him again, he would vote for him any time, because this was a man who was a credit to his country. He knew that any man who had been a soldier would understand, and he had no apology to make. He could have added that he even persuaded his mother to vote for this man—the first and last time in her life she had ever voted for a Republican.

It was a dramatic speech.

It was the first sample of similar-style speeches he would make from the rear of railroad trains all across the country when he was angry in 1948.

Reaction to that speech was enthusiastic.

The former soldiers not only understood, they applauded. Some seventy of them, who served with Truman during the war, took out a newspaper ad which said:

SHAME! SHAME!

That the public shall know, and not be led astray by the falsehoods and lies that have been broadcasted in this campaign for Eastern Judge of this County's Court, we the undersigned enlisted men of the 129th Field Artillery take this means of informing the public that Harry S. Truman was the best liked and most beloved Captain, in France or elsewhere.

We unanimously endorse him as a man, officer and gentleman, worthy of anyone's support.

The ad went on to say that Truman was a fearless man who shared both the hardships and the actual conflict with his men, and would not send any man anywhere he himself would not go; an officer who combined "executive ability with absolutely fair and impartial treatment, regardless of creed and nationalities"; a gentleman, courteous, cool and collected, "ever ready to listen to the soldier's 'Tale of Woe' with that lovable, understanding, quizzical smile of his."

The ad then listed the names of the seventy soldiers and added, " . . . we wish to let those who can vote for him know that HARRY S. TRUMAN is for every principle of life that is Just, Square and Right."

Finally, the ad featured a large reproduction of the silver loving cup they had presented to Truman after the war in "appreciation for his Justice, Ability and Leadership."

That ad had considerable impact among former soldiers.

And even though his public speaking ability was still poor, he talked with such sincerity and made such good sense that people listened.

In one of his speeches, reprinted with his picture in the

Independence *Examiner,* Truman said that road spending should be put on a sound budget basis "with a certain amount per mile for upkeep on dirt roads and a certain amount per mile for upkeep on rock roads, and then what was left . . . used for building permanent highways.

"I want men for road overseers who know roads and who want to work—men who will do a day's work for a day's pay, who will work for the county as they would for themselves. I would rather have forty men for overseers who are willing to work than to have sixty politicians who care nothing about work."

These were dangerous words for a Pendergast-supported candidate when everybody knew that most of the road jobs were primarily political appointments.

"I believe that honest work for the county is the best politics today," said Truman.

Any political candidate seeks support wherever he can find it. Truman expected—and received—support based on the fact that he was a well-known member of the Masons. Membership in any Masonic Lodge had strong meaning in that area.

Something even more significant at that time was the increasing political strength of the Ku Klux Klan. Some close friends of Truman's even felt it might be politically expedient to become a member of the Klan, but he refused. The Ku Klux Klan, wearing white hoods and burning fiery crosses, were men banded together because of their hate of minority groups. No Klan member could ever give a Catholic a job. "I won't agree to anything like that," Truman reportedly said. "I had a Catholic battery in the war and if any of those boys need help, I'm going to give them jobs." Besides, Truman had a vivid boyhood memory: "I can never forget the look on the faces of Negroes I saw in flight from a burning cross in Independence."

Ku Klux Klan opposition hurt him, and the Independence *Examiner* called the primary "the hottest fight in the history of the county, and in many ways the cleanest. There was some trouble at the polls, although an ugly situation was narrowly averted at Fairmount Junction after the polls had closed."

The election was kept clean by many of Truman's army buddies who acted as poll watchers to make sure none of the opposition tried to change or steal votes. The "ugly situation" was just that—an attempt to steal a ballot box from the polling place and stuff it with more votes for the opposing candidate. The vote was obviously so close that such a steal might make the difference.

Some tough-looking men arrived in four taxicabs, walked up to the polling place to "borrow" the ballot box. But the leader found a 45-caliber gun poked into his stomach, heard the trigger cocked and then the firm voice of one of Truman's army buddies say, "Come on boys, let's go."

The men left in a hurry and there was no further trouble. The votes were counted as cast and Truman barely won by 282 votes.

The Truman campaign had cost $524.80 and Truman's salary as county judge would be $300 a month.

Since Jackson County was normally Democratic, any victory in the Democratic primary almost automatically meant a victory during the actual election. And so it was with Harry Truman. In his final election statement, he said, "I have made no promises to anybody or to any organization.

The support I received was wonderful and I appreciate it every bit. I shall endeavor to so serve as county judge that no man or woman will be ashamed of having voted for me, and to give a square deal to everybody and to keep the only promises I made which were made in my speeches to the public."

For the embittered opposition boss, Truman's election meant the loss of road jobs for many of his men. His comment to the press reflected this feeling: "The voters preferred a busted merchant to a prosperous banker."

Perhaps the people voted for the "busted merchant" because they could identify with his problems more easily. In those days of economic depression, people could sympathize and understand more quickly the man who had lived through the time of trouble. Prosperous bankers belonged to another breed.

Harry Truman kept his promises to the people. He visited every county institution for the aged, the indigent, the insane, checked their budgets, their living conditions, their diets and tried to improve them. He spent considerable time with the county lawyers learning the procedure under state law, and then started to cut the huge county debt. He made himself familiar with every bridge and road throughout the area.

For Harry Truman, the future now looked unexpectedly bright. He had a job of public responsibility, a job in which he took pride, and it was a job with a future. His dream then was that someday, if he worked hard enough, long enough, well enough, the people might even elect him to Congress.

Other good things were also happening: he had become

a deputy grand master of his Masonic District, a lieutenant colonel in the National Guard and an evening student at the Kansas City Law School. At the age of forty, he finally learned how to swim and, much more important, he became a father of his first and only child—Mary Margaret Truman.

With his first term almost finished, the Kansas City *Star* —a Republican paper and always violently anti-Pendergast —still had friendly words for Truman in their issue of August 3, 1924:

> The present county court is busy paying off the debt. It paid off more than $600,000 last year. It has improved the roads. It has money in the treasury. That is the difference between county courts. The men who did this, Judge McElroy and Judge Truman, are up for renomination. Tuesday, the Democratic voters of Jackson County will show whether they are interested enough in good service to renominate the men who are responsible for the remarkable showing made.

The people did just that in the Democratic primary. They renominated him for county judge despite the fact that the Ku Klux Klan had announced itself as "unalterably opposed to Harry Truman."

"They threatened to kill me," Truman said. "And I went out to one of their meetings and dared them to try. I poured it into them. Then I came down from the platform and walked through them to my car."

Waiting there were a bunch of his old, loyal army buddies, all properly armed, ready for anything that might happen.

"It was a good thing they did not come earlier," said Truman. "If they had met up with the Klan, there would have been trouble."

But the Klan opposition proved critical during the election. Normally a Republican candidate in the heavily Democratic Jackson County wouldn't stand a chance. But this time, the Republican candidate not only had the complete support of the Ku Klux Klan, but also the added support of all the anti-Pendergast Democrats. They all combined to defeat Harry Truman by 867 votes.

Now here he was, a man forty years old, and again another door had been slammed in his face.

☆   ☆   ☆   ☆   ☆

5

POLITICAL BOSS TOM PENDERGAST HELPED make Kansas City great. In doing this, however, he made the city more attractive to gamblers, made his own agreements with incoming gangsters and put millions of dollars of graft into his private pocket. He was a political boss because he could control large numbers of votes in every election. He could control these votes because his lieutenants offered help to the poor people. They got jobs for those without work, provided food for the hungry, picnics for the women and children, Christmas baskets and toys during the holidays, and they did small political favors in times of trouble. In return, the poor and grateful citizens voted for almost anybody Boss Pendergast wanted.

Despite his enormous political power, Boss Pendergast had his headquarters on the second floor of an old brick building above a café and linen store situated in a poor part of town.

Up some rickety stairs was a waiting room filled with hard chairs and old furniture. But the chairs were seldom empty. Filling them were people who wanted favors: everybody from a mother whose son was in trouble with the law to important-looking men who wanted to be elected to some political office.

One day in 1926 Harry Truman sat on one of those hard chairs.

Since his previous political defeat, he had stayed out of politics for several years. Whether or not Truman had money or luck, and no matter how poor his prospects, he always did have one important thing—friends. Jackson County was filled with friends who liked Harry Truman, who worried about him, who wanted to help him.

Some of them helped him get a job as a salesman for the Kansas City Automobile Club. He did surprisingly well. Within a year he sold more than a thousand memberships, and his self-confidence grew stronger.

Other friends offered him a chance to help them start a new building and loan association, and they named Truman as general manager.

Still other friends told him about a bank they could buy cheap, and without any cash down payment. Was he interested? Yes, indeed he was. He still had huge debts to pay off on his haberdashery store and he was interested in any proposition that might mean money. But the bank they bought was ready to go broke, and they sold it fast.

It was at this time that his political friend Mike Pendergast told him about the upcoming election that year. One of the available jobs was that of county collector, and it paid twenty-five thousand dollars a year in salary and fees. With that kind of money he could quickly clear his debts.

But in order to get the Democratic nomination for that job, Truman first had to get the personal approval of the boss, Tom Pendergast. And that's why he was sitting there that day on that hard chair in the waiting room.

Before Tom Pendergast saw Truman, he first said to one of his lieutenants, "My nephew Jim is bringing this man Truman to see me. Jim thinks he has a future. What kind of guy is he?"

The man praised Truman highly, mentioned his many friends. Boss Pendergast was not impressed, and asked, "He is ornery, isn't he?"

Pendergast had a point. Truman was friendly rather than charming, a man of practical intelligence rather than brilliance. He seemed plain, neat, undistinguished, aware of his own limitations. He was obviously honest and sincere, a hard worker who seemed to get along well with everybody. Most important of all, for Pendergast, Harry Truman was extremely loyal to his friends.

This loyalty was at that time of great political help, but the time would come when it would also hurt him deeply.

When Truman walked into Boss Pendergast's inner office, he found himself in a small room, barely twelve feet square, with an old rolltop desk, a brass cuspidor, a few chairs and a worn rug. Boss Pendergast was sitting in his swivel chair, his body looking like a barrel, his black derby still cocked on his huge bald head. His face had a growing look of impatience while he waited for people to ask their favors.

Harry Truman asked his political favor and Boss Pendergast growled and said no.

Pendergast then explained why. He had promised the job of county collector to somebody else. However, if Truman was interested, he would support him for the position of presiding judge of the County Court. This judgeship offered much more prestige, but much less salary.

What should he do? His debts were on his mind. He needed money more than prestige. And yet this was an important public job. It controlled a multimillion-dollar budget and some nine hundred jobs. Truman thought it over, then accepted the Pendergast offer.

This election was easier. By this time, the fanatic Ku Klux Klan had lost most of its political zing. As for the opposition Democratic leaders, Pendergast had set up a hard, fixed arrangement sharing the prize political jobs. Truman won that election in 1926 by sixteen thousand votes.

He later defended his relations with Boss Pendergast by saying that every Democratic politician in Missouri went to Pendergast for support; that Pendergast was always helping people, even those who did nothing for him; and that you could trust Tom Pendergast because his word was his bond.

Of course, Boss Pendergast wasn't simply doing Harry Truman a favor—he expected something in return: Truman's cooperation as to which people he picked for the nine hundred jobs.

But what Pendergast told Truman was this: "Pick our people for the key jobs, but if they don't work well, then fire them and hire others."

Truman took Pendergast at his word. He hired them, then soon fired most of them "in the county's interest."

In the county's interest, Truman also cut the number of road overseers from sixty to sixteen, stopped their expense accounts and set up a strict system of bookkeeping inspection, "which gave the crooked contractors an awful pain."

When Truman took it over, the road system was a wreck,

the courthouse almost falling down, the county finances in such a poor state that there was almost no money to care for the poor, the aged and the mentally sick.

Here was Harry Truman's chance to prove himself a different kind of a hero, a civic hero.

First he hired the two best engineers he could find. He didn't care about their politics, and they turned out to be a Democrat and a Republican. These two top engineers proposed a program of two hundred and twenty-four miles of new roads to cost an estimated six and a half million dollars.

This was big money for any county, especially one that already lacked money for so many other things. The only way to get such money was to ask the public to approve a bond issue.

"You can't do it," Pendergast told Truman. "They'll say I'm going to steal it." Pendergast added that other county judges for the past twenty years had tried unsuccessfully to do the same thing. But Truman insisted that he could do it, that he could go to the people and explain that they needed the roads to give the farmers better transportation to the towns, and to give the towns a closer connection to each other. All Pendergast would finally say was that Truman could tell the voters anything he wanted, but he said it with a growl and almost a sneer.

A less stubborn man might have dropped the plan right then. Not Truman. He accepted it as a challenge.

After all, he had recruited volunteers for the National Guard, he had sold shirts and ties at his haberdashery store, sold himself as a political candidate, sold memberships in an automobile club—why couldn't he sell an idea he believed in, a program of action he deeply felt would help the public?

He did just that. He went to the people in every town and village in the county. He told them how new roads would improve real estate values, new roads would open up scenic and recreational areas, new roads would give farmers quicker outlets for their produce. But the one thing he said, again and again, that seemed to stir the most people was his solemn promise to give contracts only to the lowest bidders.

In effect, what he was saying was that he would keep the roads out of politics, that Boss Pendergast would not dip his fat finger into the contracts and profits of these roads. For a simple presiding judge, this was a strong statement to make—and mean.

But Truman did make it and he did mean it, and the people believed him. They voted to approve the bond issue for his roads.

Truman's nonpartisan engineers wanted further assurance that Pendergast would not interfere politically. They went to see him. With his usual growl, Pendergast told them that he had promised Truman he would leave him alone, and he intended to do just that.

Then it came down to cases. Truman's first road-building contract went to the low bidder, a man in South Dakota. The local contractors, favored till now, screamed. Boss Pendergast then invited Truman to meet with them, and he recognized many of the crooked contractors who had been involved in previous road scandals.

"These boys tell me that you won't give them contracts," said Pendergast.

"They can get them," said Truman, "if they are the low bidders, but they won't get paid unless they come up to specifications."

Truman never forgot the next thing Pendergast told the contractors: "Didn't I tell you boys, he's the contrariest cuss in Missouri?"

Pendergast not only refused to put pressure on Truman to favor his contractors, but he also refrained from using indirect pressure on the two other county judges to outvote Truman. And the strange thing, the thing hard to believe, was that Pendergast, a secret partner of three of the contractors at that meeting, stood to lose considerable money because of Truman's stubborn honesty. Yet he told Truman, "You carry out the agreement you made with the people of Jackson County."

And so it was. The roads were built by the lowest bidders, and according to plan. As a result, Jackson County had the best roads, at the least cost per mile, of almost any county in the United States, "except Westchester County in New York."

And why did Pendergast permit it?

Truman had his own answer: "Pendergast would stay with his friends, straight or crooked."

The anti-Pendergast, Republican newspaper, the Kansas City *Star*, stood by him, too:

> Judge Truman has been extraordinarily efficient in supervising the expenditure of the 6½ million dollar bond issue on

county roads; not a suspicion of graft has developed. He has been an earnest advocate of simplified county government and of regional county planning.

The *Star* even supported Truman for re-election in 1930 against a "high-class man" who was the Republican candidate. Before doing this, the *Star* had put Truman through a long period of testing.

A Kansas City *Star* reporter remembered that it was part of his job to knock Judge Truman out of bed every morning at three o'clock, without fail, with a telephone question. It wasn't ever the same question, but it was always a specific question about the county and its affairs as formulated and handed to him by the night managing editor.

"He was always polite," said the reporter of Truman, "always patient and always gave me an answer. I wouldn't have stood for it, but he did. That was about the time I decided this Judge Truman had something special on the ball."

Truman was more than just a presiding judge now; he was the political leader of eastern Jackson County. Mike Pendergast had died, and Tom had turned over the county control to Truman, who was highly effective as a political leader. In any election Truman could safely deliver some eleven thousand votes. Unlike Pendergast, Truman did not have to buy his votes or steal them. Pendergast lieutenants often hired people to vote as "repeaters"—vote many times for the same candidate in the same election in different polling places. The voters in Truman's county voted for Truman's candidates because they believed in Truman. He had kept his promises, and nobody questioned his honesty.

Somebody asked Truman how such a clean-minded man as he could keep such close company with the corrupt Pendergast machine.

His answer was that he owed his political life to the Pendergast organization, that he never would have had an opportunity to have a career in politics without its support. To be sure, the organization did things he believed wrong, but he also felt the best way to help clean up an organization was from the inside, not the outside. If he tried to wreck the organization that launched him, he said, people would call him an ungrateful yellow dog, and they would be right. In spite of everything else, he felt that the top people of the Pendergast machine had been his loyal friends. Loyalty to friends had always been one of Truman's strongest characteristics.

But politics had taken an ugly tone in Kansas City. Elections had become more bitter and bloody. Election workers opposed to Pendergast were beaten with blackjacks and baseball bats, and gangsters roamed the streets with machine guns. In one election opposition gangsters even threatened to kidnap Truman's six-year-old daughter.

In fact, the tenor of the whole country had changed. The high wave of general prosperity had suddenly ended, plunging the people into panic. The stock market on Wall Street completely collapsed in 1929, and thousands of businesses all over the country shut up shop. Millions of Americans suddenly found themselves without jobs, without money, without food, without hope.

Truman saw all this during a twenty-four-thousand-mile automobile trip. He was touring the country, at his own expense, inspecting county courthouses before deciding on

71

the kind he wanted for Kansas City. That proposed courthouse was part of a ten-year plan he had proposed in another fifty-million-dollar bond issue which he had helped
pass.

But this American tour was much more than a tour of
civic buildings. Truman saw the problems of a people in
trouble, a people in the depths of depression, one third of
a nation ill-fed, ill-housed, ill-clothed. He saw hungry children, men, desperate for any job, selling apples on the
streets, women on bread lines, slums and shantytowns unfit
even for animals to live in. These were the kind of memories that shaped Harry Truman's mind at a critical point
in his life. They were the kind of memories that deepened
his sense of dedication to public service.

Franklin D. Roosevelt had seen these same things, and
had also been affected by them. Roosevelt was then governor of New York, and a strong Democratic candidate for
the presidency. Truman had attended the Democratic National Convention in Chicago in 1932 when Roosevelt was
nominated.

President Harding had died while in office and Calvin
Coolidge had succeeded him. Coolidge was a thin, quiet
man, who had served as President during an era of high
prosperity, but he did not choose to run again. The
American people then elected another Republican, Herbert
Hoover, as their new President. It was at the end of Hoover's
term that the Wall Street stock market crashed and the
depression and the panic came. By now the country cla-
mored for a change and elected Franklin D. Roosevelt, a
Democrat, as President.

Truman became an enthusiastic supporter of Roosevelt's.

In an attempt to create work for the unemployed he set up a program called the Works Projects Administration. Truman served in this WPA, without salary, as the federal re-employment director for Missouri. Here was a chance to do something specific to help more people, for Truman knew what it meant to be broke, to need money and hope. Nor could he forget the desperation he had seen on so many faces during his nation-wide tour.

At this time, Truman was elected head of a regional organization to plan civic improvements for nearby counties in Missouri and Kansas. He also became a director of the National Conference on City Planning, and president of the National Old Trains Association, a group concerned with building first-class highways over historic trails.

Truman was now gaining a wider reputation in Missouri. The Odessa County *Democrat* editorially launched a Truman for Governor boom; however, Boss Pendergast had another candidate for that position.

Truman now had another dream—more than anything else, he wanted to be a Congressman. But Boss Pendergast had his own candidate for that job, too.

Truman had not managed to save much money on his job as presiding judge, which paid less than six thousand dollars a year. He knew, too, that Pendergast made it a point to rotate this job also, and so it seemed highly unlikely that he could run for re-election in 1934. He was fifty years old that year. He had a growing girl, growing needs, and unpaid debts that traced back to the haberdashery store. As he looked into his future again, he saw himself side-tracked to some minor county office, with eventual retirement into oblivion.

In 1934 Boss Pendergast was in trouble. Kansas City gangsters operated too openly; graft and corruption were too obvious. Throughout the state there was a growing reaction against Pendergast.

One of his few political defeats had been the election to the United States Senate, two years before, of Bennett Champ Clark. Clark had fought Pendergast on the "boss" issue, and won. Now Clark had announced in Washington that he would not only name the new Democratic senatorial candidate in 1934, but that he would again beat Pendergast. Most state politicians agreed that if Clark could do this, he would surely replace Pendergast as the most important political figure in Missouri.

Pendergast knew all this. He also knew that the candidate he selected had to have a record completely clean of any hint of corruption, plus a record of proven independence within the Pendergast organization.

Pendergast offered the senatorial nomination to several men, but they all refused it. None of them seemed to want to get involved in a tough primary fight, tied to Pendergast, when the prime issue would be "bossism."

It was only then that Pendergast listened to his nephew Jim, who strongly recommended Truman for the Senate seat.

Jim Pendergast summed up his reasons: Truman was a war veteran with an excellent record and many friends, a Missouri farmer, a high official in the Masons, an active American Legion member, a highly successful judge. Most of all, he was so honest, so clean of corruption, that even the anti-Pendergast Kansas City *Star* had never been able to dig up anything against him. Still another strong plus in favor of Truman was his outspoken support of President Roosevelt, which would help greatly at this peak time of Roosevelt's popularity.

In his first two years of office, Roosevelt had told the American people that "the only thing to fear is fear itself." Proclaiming a New Deal for the American people, Roosevelt pushed through a series of reforms and projects which helped instill a new spirit of confidence in the country. The Works Projects Administration made work for the jobless, the Civilian Conservation Corps took young men off the streets and put them to work in reclamation projects in the forests. A federal deposit insurance program renewed public confidence in banks, a federal loan program helped tide over the farmers in their time of trouble, more food was made available to the hungry, and a social security system was set up to provide for the aged.

Truman had publicly approved of all these things, which was very much in his favor, and he had another final advantage: In Missouri, the tradition had been for its two Senators to represent the two parts of the state. Senator Clark was from St. Louis; the Republican Senator against whom Truman might run was also from St. Louis, while Truman, of course, was from the western part of the state.

Pendergast listened to all these arguments and finally agreed to accept Truman.

Truman listened to the offer without enthusiasm. He explained his reluctance. He felt he wasn't well enough known in the state to win, and that he personally couldn't afford the cost of such a campaign.

But he was persuaded to run and said later, "I never ran for an office I really wanted."

On May 14, 1934, at 4:00 A.M., Harry Truman wrote a private memo to himself:

"Now I am a candidate for the United States Senate. If the Almighty God decides that I go there, I am going to pray, as King Solomon did, for wisdom to do the job."

It was a rough race. Truman's two opponents in the Democratic primary included a successful seven-term Congressman, Jacob L. Milligan, who had the firm backing of Senator Clark; and another Congressman, John L. Cochran, who had been voted by Washington correspondents as "one of the six most useful members of the House," and had the support of the mayor of St. Louis.

As far as principles and issues were concerned, all three men were of a similar stripe. All were liberal, all were strongly pro-Roosevelt. But Truman's two opponents had an issue that he didn't have: bossism. Both men hit hard at Truman, called him "Uncle Tom's boy." The St. Louis *Post-Dispatch* hit even harder, calling him, "Tom's errand boy." The phrase stuck. Boss Pendergast himself told a St. Louis *Post-Dispatch* reporter that he had noticed that there were United States Senators representing oil and steel and the railroads and so he had decided to send his "office boy" to represent Pendergast.

On the other hand, Truman neither denied nor minimized his connection with Pendergast. And Pendergast did produce the final vote from Kansas City and Jackson County that elected Truman by forty thousand votes. Two years later, an honest election commission purged the Kansas City voting registration lists of more than sixty thousand "ghosts." These were Pendergast-produced votes, using names taken from cemeteries, names of people supposedly living in empty lots, names of voters found underage or otherwise unqualified, names of large numbers of people claiming to live in a small single house, and names of people voting as many as thirty times in that single election.

While these "ghosts" helped elect Truman, it is true that a large slice of the lopsided vote for Cochran, his opponent in St. Louis, was also a "ghost" vote. Probably, if all the ghosts had been killed off on all sides, and if the boss-controlled votes of both cities were somehow eliminated, Harry Truman would still have won because of his huge vote in the rural areas.

Sounding a warning note to Pendergast, Kansas City's federal district attorney, Maurice Milligan, brother of one of the defeated candidates, said, "The dishonest ballot, if continued, will destroy this government. I believe the man who perpetrates that practice upon the people should be treated as any other criminal. He not only violates the laws of that state, but he also violates the federal laws."

Pendergast couldn't care less; he was still crowing over his victory. When a *Post-Dispatch* reporter asked him, "Do you exact any promises in advance?" Pendergast answered: "If a candidate hasn't got enough sense to see who helped him win and hasn't sense enough to recognize that man's friends, there is no use asking for favors from that candidate in advance."

The Kansas City *Star* sounded the victory note: "Tom Pendergast today stands forth as the undisputed dictator of Missouri's democracy. . . . To jump a man from a county court bench to a Senate nomination was quite an undertaking. . . ."

But on its editorial page, the *Star* gave Truman his due:

There were other factors, of course. The attractive personality of Judge Truman was a real asset, and there was weight to the feeling that it would be unfair that the eastern end of the state should have both United States Senators.

While Judge Truman is not well known throughout the state, he is favorably known in Kansas City. As presiding judge of the county court, he has made a good record. Jackson County has found him a capable and honest public official.

The St. Louis *Post-Dispatch* was more bitter about it, editorializing that the "obscure" Truman was the Democratic nominee "because Tom Pendergast willed it so."

Pendergast accepted the credit and told a reporter, "Frankly, it was a matter of pride to me to name just any man and beat Clark's candidate."

After that hot primary, the actual election was an anti-climax. In that Roosevelt year, a whole host of Democrats were swept into office. Truman won easily by more than two hundred and sixty thousand votes.

But the heavy hand of Pendergast in that election gave the victory a sour smell nationally. It would take all of Truman's stubborn persistence to fight the feeling that he was simply a Pendergast messenger boy.

His daughter Margaret, then not quite eleven years old, cried at the news because, she said, "I don't want to go to that mean old Washington."

Later, when she quieted down, she asked her father, "What's a Senator?"

It was a good question, and it would take Harry Truman a long time to learn the full weight of the answer.

☆ ☆ ☆ ☆ ☆ **6**

HARRY TRUMAN HAD NO ILLUSIONS ABOUT himself when he first went to Washington as a United States Senator.

He later confessed that he was as timid as a country boy arriving on the campus of a great university for his first year. He introduced himself to a Washington correspondent of the Kansas City *Journal Post* as "only a humble member of the next Senate, green as grass and ignorant as a fool about practically everything worth knowing."

Reporting to the Kansas City Elks Club, he flatly admitted that he hardly hoped to rate with the great Missouri Senators of the past, but that he would do his best to keep his feet on the ground because he was "just a farmer boy from Jackson County."

One newspaper mocked his speech, editorializing that Truman "is not moved as yet by the splendors of Washington or the majesty of the Senate."

They were wrong. Truman was much moved. With his mind steeped in his country's history, and the full knowledge of the Senate's past and potential, he felt so inadequate that he planned to enroll in the night law school of Georgetown University to finish an education he had never completed.

79

Pendergast himself had given Truman some curt advice: "Work hard, keep your mouth shut and answer your mail."

However, in those early days, the Pendergast shadow hung over Truman like a heavy cloud. He had difficulty recruiting qualified assistants, who felt their reputations would suffer from such association. One who later did work for Truman recorded his first impression of the man: "Here was a guy—a punk—sent up by gangsters." He soon changed his mind, and confided, "I realized that my original impression of him was all wet. This was a man of real integrity and brains—and no Pendergast or anyone else was going to push him around."

The Senate assigned him desk Number 94, almost at the end of the back row. Another former county judge, Senator Hamilton Lewis of Illinois, tried to help him. Lewis, who was then the minority leader of the Senate, told Truman, "Don't start out with an inferiority complex. For the first six months, you'll wonder how you got here. After that, you'll wonder how the rest of us got here."

Other Senators also helped him. Bennett Clark, his Missouri colleague, forgot the bitterness of the previous campaign, and introduced him to other Senators. He showed him the barber shop where Senators get free haircuts, the bath house and the gym, and gave him some valuable hints.

Senator Carl Hayden of Arizona taught Truman the technicalities and customs of Senate procedure, and Vice-President John Nance Garner, presiding officer of the Senate, quickly became his good friend and adviser. Many of the other Senators soon warmed to Truman. His smile was always friendly and sincere and he seemed full of an eager willingness to learn and work.

Truman later admitted that his attitude toward others came from something he had learned as a teen-ager, something that nobody had taught him. He used to watch his mother and father closely to learn what he could do to please them, and he did the same thing with his schoolteachers and playmates. He found that if he really made a strong effort to get along with his associates, he usually was able to get what he wanted. He found this method was highly successful on the farm, in school, in the Army—and particularly in the Senate.

A Senate custom assigns every freshman Senator to two important committees and also some minor ones. The important ones for Truman were the Appropriations Committee and the Interstate Commerce Committee. Appropriations concerned itself with government expenses, the making and unmaking of national budgets; Interstate Commerce concentrated on the country's transportation, everything from highways to railroads. Both committees proved an invaluable experience to him.

Truman later explained that the real work of a Senator was done in committee rather than on the floor of the Senate, that some committee projects require years of study, research correspondence and hearings, and that these activities are never published in the *Congressional Record*. But he made it his business to master all the details of any project confronting a committee of which he was a member.

That put it most mildly. The main project of the Interstate Commerce Committee at that time was an investigation of railroad finances. A subcommittee of six had been assigned the study. Truman wasn't even on it, but he did his own research, reading some fifty books on railroad prob-

81

lems. As the subject grew more complex, and the hearings went on endlessly, one subcommittee member dropped out and Truman was assigned to it. Since he seemed to know more than anyone else, and since he was often the only committee member at the hearings, he was made vice-chairman of the subcommittee.

The little boy who had watched and loved trains, the young man who had worked as a timekeeper on the Santa Fe Railroad, now became the country's most important pair of ears listening to the problems of the nation's railroads.

"The public's indifference to the hearings was simply deafening," wrote one reporter. But if the public didn't seem to care, the railroads did. When the case of the bankrupt Missouri Pacific Railroad came up for committee investigation, the railroad put enormous pressure on Truman to soft-pedal or sidetrack the investigation of his home state railroad. Truman refused. He told his staff, "Don't ease up on anything. Treat this investigation just as you do all the others."

"There were not two other Senators who would have withstood such political pressure as Senator Truman did," said his chief committee assistant Max Lowenthal.

That investigation of the Missouri Pacific revealed everything from crooked stock transactions to fake bookkeeping. After two years of hearings on many railroads, the final result was a new Transportation Act, rewriting the laws on railroad operations.

Truman had followed Pendergast's advice and kept his mouth shut during the early months of his first Senate term. "I'm not going to demagogue until I have something to demagogue about," he told a friend. That time came in his report on the railroad hearings, when he told the Senate, "Some of the greatest railroads have been deliberately looted by their financial agents. . . . When one of these great transportation companies fails . . . they get all the flesh and the stockholders and public get the bones. . . ."

It was one of the strange facts of history that the Transportation Act, which Truman helped to shape, became the law which he would put into full force for the first time as President of the United States to avoid a nation-wide railroad crisis in 1947.

One of Truman's firm friends in the Senate was Arthur Vandenberg of Michigan, a leading Republican. Once, when Vandenberg presided over the Senate in Garner's absence, he called on Truman for his comment on some floor discussion. After Truman made his statement, Vandenberg told the rest of the Senate: "When the Senator from Missouri makes a statement like that, we can take it for the truth."

That was a remark Truman never forgot.

One of the bills Truman supported was the Public Utility Holding Company Act, which gave the government greater control over the rates which power utilities charged the public. The utilities organized a huge mail campaign, and Truman received some thirty thousand letters asking him to vote against the bill. He burned them all.

The Kansas City *Star* reported that Pendergast often sent Truman telegrams urging him to vote a certain way on a certain issue, but that Truman had said, "I don't follow his advice on legislation. I vote the way Missourians as a whole would want me to vote."

It took courage to buck the boss and the big lobbies.

This was all part of the hard core of the man. No matter how big he became, he never forgot his roots. He never forgot his struggles as a small farmer and a small businessman in a small town.

Again and again, in speeches and statements, he expressed his personal philosophy that he would rather see a thousand insurance companies with four million dollars in assets than one insurance company with four billion dollars; a hundred steel companies rather than one United States Steel Corporation; a thousand banks rather than one National City Bank.

He also said repeatedly that he felt a thousand county seat towns of seven thousand people each were a thousand times more important to our country than one city of seven million people.

Back home, his mother subscribed to the *Congressional Record*, the daily recording of everything said and done in Congress. When her son Harry said or did anything of which she approved, she let him know; when he did something of which she did *not* approve, she also let him know. Truman was grateful for her private opinions, suggestions, criticisms and pressure.

But there was a single case of pressure from Boss Pendergast which he did not appreciate.

The Senate was then voting on its choice for majority leader between Senator Pat Harrison of Mississippi and Senator Alben Barkley of Kentucky. Truman had committed his vote to Harrison, but the Roosevelt administration preferred Barkley. Since the vote was close, the Roosevelt administration tried every means to persuade Senators to vote for Barkley.

Truman got a call from Pendergast. "Look here, Harry,

Jim Farley just called me and asked if I couldn't talk to you about voting for Barkley. Can't you do that?"

Truman said that he couldn't, and he explained why. Pendergast understood the importance of a man's keeping his word, and he didn't press the matter. A political boss can stay in power only if he keeps his promises to his own people.

Barkley also understood, and remained Truman's friend —and later became his vice-president.

But the more Truman thought about the incident, the angrier he got. He wasn't so much irritated at Pendergast as he was angry at President Roosevelt. Why didn't the President deal with him directly? Why did the President insult his integrity by supposing that his mind was not his own, and that he could only be approached through Boss Pendergast? After all, there were few Senators who had voted for the Roosevelt New Deal more consistently than he. The Soldiers' Bonus Bill was the only one on which he had differed. The administration didn't want it—and Truman did.

As his anger increased, Truman confided to his friends that he was tired of being pushed around by the administration, tired of having the President treat him like an office boy, and he would do something about it.

He called the White House and spoke to the President's press secretary, Steve Early. He told Early that he was a United States Senator representing the state of Missouri, and he deserved the courtesy and consideration of his office from everybody, including the President of the United States. Would Early please pass this message on to the President? Early promised he would.

Harry Truman had come a long way from the shy boy with thick glasses. He had refused a direct request from Boss Tom Pendergast and he had asserted himself to the President of the United States.

He was a man with the courage of his own convictions, responsible only to himself and the public he served.

Except for some scribbled notes recommending Missouri citizens for small government jobs, Pendergast didn't bother Truman much after that.

Boss Pendergast was then busy with other things. His hobby of betting on horses had become a mania. Later records showed that he had bet two million dollars on horses in 1935, and lost some $600,000. To keep himself in money, Pendergast accepted a fat bribe of almost a half million dollars from some insurance companies in return for his special influence in returning to them from the state some ten million dollars. And the newly elected Governor Lloyd C. Stark, whom Pendergast had helped elect, now turned on him and started a detailed investigation of the Pendergast political machine. Headed by federal attorney Maurice Milligan, brother of the man whom Truman had defeated for Senator, the investigation concentrated on vote fraud and later revealed some sixty thousand "ghost votes," votes recorded for people who were either dead or non-existent. It resulted in two and hundred fifty-nine convictions and the elimination of these "ghost votes" from the registration books.

Truman called these convictions "a persecution of innocent men and women," and told the Senate "that a Jackson County Missouri Democrat has as much chance of a fair trial in the Federal District Court of western Missouri as a Jew would have in a Hitler court. . . ." Truman made this speech voicing his opposition to the reappointment of Maurice Milligan as United States District Attorney, and explained that his opposition to Milligan began long before vote frauds were brought to light in Kansas City, that Milligan's morals and political thinking never did appeal to him.

The Kansas City judge presiding at the election trials denounced Truman's Senate speech as "the speech of a man nominated by ghost votes, elected with ghost votes, and whose speeches are probably written by ghost writers." The St. Louis *Post-Dispatch* also ridiculed the speech in a cartoon showing Truman as a dummy on a ventriloquist's lap.

That speech marked Truman's low point in the Senate. For years he had worked hard to earn the respect of his fellow Senators, and most of them had accepted him. Now, because of this speech, many of them again regarded him as "Tom's boy."

Federal attorney Maurice Milligan, after his full investigation of the Pendergast corruption, admitted, "At no time did the finger of suspicion ever point in the direction of Harry Truman."

Noted liberal Senator, independent Republican George Norris, had said of Truman, "I watched him in the public service more than I otherwise would, and I must say that in all the time I knew him, I never knew of an instance, I never knew of one time that the bosses or machine controlled his official work."

His record of honesty and independence was clean. Even

his political opposition admitted that. Then why would he make such a speech that would again taint him with the stamp of suspicion?

His was a simple answer: loyalty.

Things got worse. Federal investigators discovered a huge bribe that Pendergast had not reported on his income tax. Pendergast was arrested, brought to trial and convicted. Some of Truman's best friends now urged him to denounce Pendergast.

Truman refused. "Tom Pendergast has always been my friend," he said, "and I won't desert a sinking ship."

That took considerable courage. His first Senate term was almost over and it seemed political suicide to tie himself up with the stamp of proven Pendergast corruption. He had an easy way out, and he refused to take it. It was more than mere loyalty for Truman—it was now a point of honor.

Once he made his statement, his political friends saw it as the end of his political career, and they told him so. President Roosevelt sent Truman a message that if he would drop out of the upcoming Senate race, Roosevelt would appoint him to a highly paid job on the Interstate Commerce Commission. Truman's friends urged him to accept. They pointed out that the broken Pendergast machine could hardly give him too much support, that Missouri's big city newspapers were all against him, that his two political opponents for the Senate—Governor Lloyd Stark and Maurice Milligan—were both highly popular, that the St. Louis political machine of Mayor Bernard Dickmann favored Stark and the personal political machine of Senator Bennett Clark favored Milligan. They pointed out that he had no campaign funds, no political organization, no single piece of legislation with his name on it.

"I'm whipped," Truman told a friend. "This is the end of me."

But his assistant, Victor Messall, went to see Truman's old friend Jim Pendergast, who still held together the remnants of his uncle's political machine. Messall asked him if he would support Truman if he ran.

"Tell Harry," said Jim Pendergast, "that if he gets only two votes, those two will be mine and my wife's."

Messall then called Truman, urging him to file for the senatorial nomination. "If you don't run, you're through in politics," he said.

Truman finally agreed to run, explaining to a friend, "I'm going to file. I wouldn't have the guts to go home and face my people if I ran out."

The St. Louis *Post-Dispatch* greeted the Truman announcement with a cartoon showing two huge trucks about to crash into each other. One truck was labeled Stark, the other Milligan, and in between was Harry Truman in a child's toy car. Underneath the cartoon, the caption said, "NO PLACE FOR A KIDDYCAR."

Almost every leading Missouri politician seemed to agree with that, and not a single one of them declared in favor of Truman.

That year of 1940 was also a presidential election year, and Franklin D. Roosevelt was running for a third term. Roosevelt had dropped Garner as Vice-President and seemed to open the field for any other candidate. Governor Stark felt he had the Roosevelt blessing for the job and a good chance of getting it, and promptly opened his convention headquarters in Chicago. But the Stark boom collapsed when Roosevelt pinpointed Henry A. Wallace for the vice-presidency.

Stark's attempt to run for both the United States Senate and the vice-presidency at the same time caused considerable resentment in Missouri. Senator Bennett Clark referred to Stark's candidacy for the vice-presidency as "ill-fated, short-lived and ludicrous."

But Stark was still heavily favored to win. Milligan's chances fizzled badly because of his poor speeches which failed to stir anybody.

Truman meanwhile started his tour of seventy-five Missouri counties, shaking all available hands, making about ten speeches a day, sleeping in the car between towns. He concentrated on the farmers, talking their language and on their own terms. The first bill Truman had introduced in the Senate provided insurance on farm mortgages by the Farm Credit Administration, and he had voted for all the things farmers wanted, from soil conservation to flood control.

Labor also moved in to help, especially the railroad unions. They appreciated what he had done for fair standards in the Transportation Act. They rated Truman as "the best friend labor ever had." They even put out a special edition of their newspaper, featuring Truman's New Deal record, and circulated more than five hundred thousand copies throughout the state.

Stark was a wealthy man, owner of the famous Stark's Delicious apple orchards, and quickly bought up billboards and radio time to publicize his cause. Truman's finances were desperate—he couldn't even prevent his mother's farm from being foreclosed. He was forced to borrow three thousand dollars on his life insurance policy to pay some of his more pressing campaign expenses. Two hundred dollars went for postage on letters making the plea, "If you want to see Harry Truman returned to the Senate, send a dollar immediately." They raised eighteen hundred dollars that way. The total Truman campaign cost about twenty thousand dollars.

Always beside him was his wife Bess. She never made any speeches herself, but she always helped him with his.

Part of a whispering campaign against Truman was the fact that he had put his wife on his Senate payroll, at a salary of thirty-five hundred dollars a year. Truman freely admitted it. Furthermore, he outlined all the work she did for him, helping with his committee work, his personal mail, his reports. He said quite honestly that he would have preferred to have her home, keeping house, rather than helping him at the office, but they needed the extra money to pay their bills.

Truman afterward called that campaign "the bitterest and dirtiest fight I ever witnessed."

Most of the dirt and bitterness came when Stark and Milligan tried to tie Truman to every piece of Pendergast corruption, and Stark was the more biting of the two. It was a political fact that Truman had introduced Stark to Pendergast, had urged Pendergast to support Stark for Governor. Pendergast had said, "He's no good, Harry," but reluctantly agreed. Truman was talking to a reporter about this and mentioned the fact that he still had a letter from Stark thanking him for the introduction to Pendergast.

The reporter asked when Truman planned to use that letter in the campaign and was startled when Truman said he didn't plan to use that letter at all because he didn't think it was the right thing to do.

Truman felt forced to open his speeches by telling his audiences, "I thought I'd come by and show you I don't have horns and a tail."

Fortunately for Truman, he got some unexpected support. Victor Messall and Senator Carl Hatch persuaded Missouri Senator Bennett Clark that the Milligan candidacy was a lost cause, and they knew he preferred Truman to Stark, and besides, Truman had once made two campaign speeches for Clark. Clark's late support for Truman had real importance.

Then Truman made two important political conquests in St. Louis: Robert Hannegan, the Number Two man in the city's Democratic machine, and Jordan Chambers, the "Black Mayor" of St. Louis, so-called because of his control of the voters in the Negro wards.

Hannegan went all out for Truman, had his precinct workers ringing doorbells, spreading the word. Chambers was a little harder to convince. He had heard about Truman's speeches on the "brotherhood of man, not merely the brotherhood of white men, but the brotherhood of all men before law." He also knew that Truman had said, ". . . numberless antagonisms and indignities heaped upon any race will eventually try human patience to the limit, and a crisis will develop. We all know the Negro is here to stay, and in no way can be removed from our political and economic life, and we should recognize his inalienable rights, as specified in our Constitution. Can any man claim protection of our laws, if he denies that protection to others?"

Chambers knew all that, but he had heard fine-sounding words before and he was much more interested in the specific action of the man. He was more interested in the fact that Truman had fired a man from his campaign headquarters because that man had objected to Negro women campaign workers using "White Toilets."

Chambers finally told Truman, "I'm for you. I'll do what I can."

That night of the August 3rd Democratic primary, Truman found himself 11,000 votes behind. "I went to bed defeated," he said.

But by morning the count had changed. He won by the slim, state-wide margin of 7,976 votes. The big surprise had come from the St. Louis area which he won by 8,411 votes. That was also the total votes provided by the Negro wards of Jordan Chambers, who had gone for Truman by two-to-one majorities. A shift of 4,000 votes might have ended his political career.

Truman then went on to win the November election much more easily and by more than 40,000 votes.

He had now been re-elected on his own. No longer could anyone call him "Tom's boy."

☆　　☆　　☆　　☆　　☆

THE WORLD HAD CHANGED A GREAT DEAL SINCE
Harry Truman first became a United States Senator. Benito
Mussolini had turned Italy into a dictatorship, Adolf Hitler
and his Nazis had done the same thing with Germany and
both dictators seemed intent on expansion. Mussolini declared war on tiny Ethiopia on October 3, 1935, and the
League of Nations seemed powerless to do anything about
it. Hitler moved into Austria in March, 1938, made a peace
pact with Stalin and his Communist Russia in August 1939
and then took a slice of Czechoslovakia. It was only when
Germany invaded Poland on September 1, 1939, that England and France finally declared war on Germany. All of
Europe then took sides and World War II had begun.

In the Far East, Japan, too, turned into a military dictatorship. The Japanese invaded China in 1937 and in September, 1940, they signed their own treaty of alliance with
the Germans.

Long before World War II started, Senator Truman told
an American Legion group in Washington that he believed
in an adequate national defense program, and that he particularly agreed with the old Puritan who prayed regularly

for protection against the Indians—but at the same time, kept his powder dry and his gun at the ready.

As the war threat came closer to this country, Congress authorized some twenty-five billion dollars to build everything from planes to war plants. What angered Truman was the obvious waste, the way money was being thrown around by the government "by the scoop shovelful."

He decided to see for himself how much waste there really was. He got into his car and made a thirty-thousand-mile trip around the country, inspecting everything from army camps to defense industries.

Truman returned to Washington an angry man. He had seen so much grasping greed, so much bungling and waste of men and money and materials that he decided to make a speech in the Senate about it.

He discussed it with his friend, Washington correspondent Bill Helm, and finally decided he should do something more important than just make a speech. He would propose that the Senate form a committee to investigate the whole defense program.

Truman prepared his program and introduced it as Resolution 71 on February, 10, 1941, explaining why he felt such a committee was so important. In the past, he said, our country had always waited for a war to end before investigating all the mistakes and the waste. After World War I there had been more than a hundred Congressional committees checking into it, with everybody blaming everybody else for things that had gone wrong. It didn't do much good, Truman said, to find out why the barn door was not locked, after the horse was stolen.

Instead of digging up dead horses after the war, he said,

here was a chance to find the mistakes while they were happening—and correct them. This would not only guarantee the government greater economy and value, he added, but it would help win the war.

The Senate listened, passed his resolution, and appointed Truman chairman of this special committee. After the seven Senators were picked for his committee, Truman went to Attorney General Robert Jackson and asked him to recommend the best investigator he had.

Jackson recommended Hugh Fulton, a big fat man with a squeaky voice. He always wore a derby hat. Truman wasn't much impressed with him, but he soon discovered that Fulton was a man with a tough mind and a firm grasp of the job to be done. The instructions Truman issued were quite simple: Get the facts, don't show anybody any favors.

The committee met regularly in Truman's private office, soon known as "Harry's doghouse." It was a big room with a high ceiling and comfortable leather chairs. On the walls were old artillery maps from Truman's Battery D days in World War I. Here the committee discussed specific subjects for investigation, then Truman assigned a subcommittee to investigate each subject. They included such items as the shortage of rubber and metals, gas rationing, shipbuilding, camp construction, farm machinery and several dozen more.

Once a project was firmly agreed on, Hugh Fulton and his staff went to work, and then reported their results to the subcommittee. The subcommittee then held its hearings, either open to the public or closed, with everybody given a chance to explain or answer the charges.

The subcommittee then presented its findings to the full

committee, headed by Truman. After discussion by all seven Senators, Truman then presented the final report of the full committee on that subject to the whole Senate.

He let it be known everywhere that the committee had no axe to grind, that they were not interested either in whitewashes or witch hunts. And he refused to be pressured —if Boss Pendergast hadn't succeeded in browbeating him, then nobody could.

But many still tried.

One company official holding defense contracts worth hundreds of millions of dollars came to complain. He literally told Truman to let him alone . . . "call off your dogs."

Truman kept his conversation curt. He simply asked, "Are the charges true or false?"

The man hemmed and hawed. When he walked into Truman's office he had been cocksure, aggressive. But when he walked out he looked whipped.

The shy boy with the thick glasses had learned how to handle anybody.

Meanwhile world war fever had worsened. Hitler's tanks and troops, after sweeping over Europe, threatened to invade England. While the United States sent England ships and supplies, she remained militarily neutral. In the Far East the Japanese were increasingly aggressive, anxious to spread their control over the entire Pacific. On December 7, 1941, which President Roosevelt called "a day that will live in infamy," the Japanese attacked Pearl Harbor, crippling half of the entire United States Navy—at the same time that Japanese envoys in Washington were still talking about peace. Immediately afterward, Japan's ally, Germany, also declared war on the United States.

For Senator Harry Truman, who attended that joint session of Congress, and heard our declaration of war on Japan, there were mixed emotions: his anger at the Japanese sneak attack, his determination that his country would win the war and his serious question about the future course of his committee.

When war came, the committee was busily preparing an annual report, heavy with criticism of our defense effort. Now came the question whether such criticism was patriotic in time of war, whether perhaps the committee should simply shut up shop.

Truman talked it over with his members and decided that what they were doing was of even greater importance now.

The Truman Committee had worked hard all along, but now the pressure was intensified. Truman found himself the focus of all kinds of complaints from all over the country.

Housewives protested the refusal of extra sugar—rationed at that time—for home canning, and former farmer Truman helped reverse that ration rule. A steel company employee wrote that he had seen fake inspections for inferior steel plates for the Navy. Truman's investigation resulted in the conviction of several company officials.

When Truman heard Air Force pilots' complaints about the B-26 bomber, he ordered his own engineering survey of the plane. It showed that the spread of the plane's wings was too short for safety. Truman told this to the head of that company, but the company official insisted that it was too late to change the plans because the plane was already in production.

Truman was blunt: He said that in that case he would recommend that no such planes be bought. The company quickly changed its plans.

Among other things the committee found billions of dollars in defense contracts being handed out to a small number of firms whose officials, or former officials, were supposedly working for the government as volunteers.

Never had Truman been as angry as when he told the press that he intended to see that no man or men made huge profits on the blood of the boys in the foxholes.

He was equally vehement when he declared that we had no right to produce pleasure cars when we needed the steel, iron, copper, glass and manpower for national defense. The automobile industry, he insisted, should be immediately converted to the production of planes, tanks, munitions and other defense material.

The voice of Harry Truman was now a national voice of the American conscience. The Senate and the American people listened to him with growing respect.

"There is no doubt," Washington columnist Marquis Childs wrote in the St. Louis *Post-Dispatch*—a newspaper which had long and bitterly attacked Truman for his Pendergast associations—"that it (the Truman Committee) has saved billions—yes, billions—of dollars."

Childs also said that of all the ninety-six Senators, Truman was "one of the most useful and at the same time one of the most forthright and most fearless. . . ."

A poll of all the Washington correspondents by *Look* Magazine named Harry Truman one of the ten most valuable men in Washington during the war—and he was the only Senator named among the ten.

"You look tired," his friend Bill Helm told him one day.

"I am, Bill," Truman said. "I'm tired as a dog and having the time of my life."

His prestige had soared not only among his fellow Senators, but also at the White House. Truman had shown President Roosevelt an advance report with major criticism of conflicting defense agencies. Roosevelt promptly combined the agencies, before Truman issued his report, and received public credit for establishing the War Production Board. Truman simply smiled and said, "That was all right with me."

Then Roosevelt planned to appoint former Governor Lloyd Stark to a high government job. Truman let it be known that this would make him most unhappy, and Roosevelt dropped the appointment.

President Roosevelt also noted in a Philadelphia speech:

"I call particular attention to the thorough and painstaking and completely nonpartisan job of that committee of the Senate which was organized and presided over by Harry Truman. The Truman Committee has done a job that will live in history as an example of honest, efficient government at work."

This was a big jump for a Missouri Senator who had come to Washington under a black cloud, and had had to wait six months before President Roosevelt would permit him to pay a courtesy visit to the White House.

Truman made his final committee report to the Senate in 1944. This committee for which the Senate had reluctantly budgeted an original fifteen thousand dollars—but added more later—had produced thirty-one reports in forty months.

Speaking of the reports, Donald Nelson, one of the top

defense officials, said, "Its criticisms have not always been gentle, but it always hurts when the doctor touches the sore spot. We have had some spots that need doctoring."

Senator Carl Hatch of New Mexico, and a member of the Truman Committee, paid this tribute to his chairman and friend on the Senate floor:

"He has led but has never driven. He has been wise, kindly, firm and courageous. Whatever the Truman Committee has accomplished is but a reflection of the integrity, wisdom and courage of the chairman, Honorable Harry S. Truman, the junior Senator from Missouri."

The nation agreed. *Time Magazine* put Truman on its cover, called his committee "the Billion-Dollar Watchdog." More and more prominent people talked of Harry Truman as a potential presidential candidate.

The war had gone well for the United States and its allies by 1944. Our troops had successfully beaten back the Germans and Italians in North Africa (from November 1942 to May 1943), swept through Sicily that summer in a campaign of just thirty-nine days, then started slowly moving up the long length of Italy in September. It was, said President Roosevelt, "the beginning of the end."

The more dramatic follow-up was the twin-pronged invasion of France: the Allied invasion of Normandy from England on D Day, June 6, 1944, and then the sudden smash at the southern coast by Allied troops coming from Italy several months later on August 15. Our Air Corps bombers were now regularly blasting Nazi defense centers; our Navy had scored an impressive number of victories over the Japanese fleet; and our soldiers and Marines, as far back as

1942, had started to push the Japanese out of their long string of conquered islands.

Mainly because the war was still going on, and there was a peace yet to be won, President Franklin D. Roosevelt decided to run for a fourth term in 1944. High Democratic party officials had helped persuade him to make this decision because they saw in him their only logical winning candidate.

President Roosevelt would have preferred to retire to the quiet of private life. The strain of three terms had taken its toll. He was obviously tired and his health was poor.

All this made the selection of a vice-presidential candidate all the more important.

A strong feel existed among top party leaders that Vice-President Henry A. Wallace should not be renominated. They insisted that Wallace had angered the South and a large part of the conservative wing of the Democratic party. They convinced Roosevelt that Wallace's name on the ticket would mean a loss of two million votes in the upcoming election.

But who should succeed Wallace?

Shortly before the Democratic National Convention in Chicago in July, 1944, President Roosevelt invited a small group of Democratic leaders to a dinner at the White House. After dinner, the group adjourned to another room and Roosevelt asked for opinions on the vice-presidency.

Several names were discussed and temporarily discarded —including Supreme Court Justice William O. Douglas— and then Robert Hannegan suggested Harry S. Truman.

Hannegan was the new national chairman of the Democratic party. It was Hannegan who had helped provide the winning margin of votes in St. Louis that re-elected Truman to the United States Senate in 1940. Afterward, Truman had arranged for Hannegan's appointment as Collector of Internal Revenue for that area. Later, when the Democratic party offered the job of national chairman to Truman, he turned it down, but recommended Hannegan, who then got it.

Roosevelt admitted Truman's excellent reputation as chairman of the Senate Committee to investigate the national defense. However, he also brought up Truman's past association with Boss Pendergast, said that he really didn't know Truman very well, and finally added that perhaps Truman was too old.

Roosevelt then asked his son-in-law John Boettiger to find a copy of the *Congressional Directory* so they could check Truman's age.

Meanwhile, all of the assembled leaders tried to persuade Roosevelt that Truman was the man who could hurt him the least. One of the stronger voices for Truman was Democratic party treasurer Ed Pauley, a wealthy California oil man and a good friend of Truman's. Pauley told party leaders, "You are not nominating a Vice-President of the United States, but a President." When Boettiger returned with the *Congressional Directory*, Pauley casually took it, put it in his lap and talked quickly of other things to distract Roosevelt.

Roosevelt finally said to Hannegan, "Bob, I think you and everyone else here want Truman."

Pauley signaled the group to leave, and when they were all out in the hall, Hannegan excused himself and went back in. When he returned, he had a piece of paper on which Roosevelt had scribbled, "Bob, it's Truman. F.D.R."

Fortunately for Truman, they never did look up his age in the *Congressional Directory*. If they had, Roosevelt might have eliminated him. Truman was then sixty, only two years younger than Roosevelt.

Roosevelt preferred to keep his decision quiet for a while. For one thing, he hated to offend anybody. Wallace talked to F.D.R. and came away with the feeling that he still had the President's support. Senator James Byrnes of South Carolina, the Director of War Mobilization, talked to F.D.R. and felt certain that Roosevelt wanted Byrnes as Vice-President. In fact, Byrnes called Truman. "Harry," he said, "the President has given me the go sign and I'm calling up to ask you to nominate me."

Truman, who had not yet heard from Hannegan or anyone else about his own nomination, told Byrnes that he would be happy to nominate him, and also help him in any way he could at the convention.

Soon, however, Truman got the word that Bob Hannegan was quietly promoting him as the vice-presidential candidate. Truman made it plain to all his friends that Hannegan was doing this without either his knowledge or his consent.

He even sought out Hannegan and told him flatly and directly that he didn't want to be Vice-President, that he didn't want to be anything except the Senator from Missouri. He stressed the insignificance of the job and added, "I bet I can go down the street and stop the first ten men I see and they can't tell me the names of two of the last ten Vice-Presidents of the United States."

To other friends, Truman was even more blunt. He told them that they were doing him a disservice to mention his name as a vice-presidential possibility, that he already had the job he wanted most of all.

He told the same thing to his Senate office staff and to his mother and family in Missouri.

If he was really reluctant, Truman had good reason. He had a true sense of importance about his contribution to the war effort as chairman of the Senate Investigating Committee. Though the vice-presidency seemed a high honor, it was mostly an empty one. The Vice-President then had no executive duties. His only official job was to preside over the Senate, but he could not enter into their discussion, could vote only in case of a tie, and whatever ruling he made could be overruled by the Senate, if they disapproved. His main job was more social, a ribbon-cutter at ceremonies, and a representative of the President at social functions. Somebody had aptly called the vice-presidency "the graveyard of politicians."

Knowing Truman's reluctance, Hannegan persuaded Roosevelt to write another note. This one said:

Dear Bob,
 You have written me about Bill Douglas and Harry Truman. I should, of course, be very glad to run with either of them and believe that either of them would bring real strength to the ticket.

Hannegan, however, was unhappy with the unexpected new reference to Douglas, and the fact that Douglas' name preceded that of Truman. He and Pauley again met Roosevelt in his private railroad car in Chicago, while it stopped en route to San Diego, just before the convention opened. They got F.D.R.'s permission then to have the letter re-written with Truman's name first. They also got his renewed assurance that he preferred Truman to Byrnes.

They did this because Truman had told Hannegan that Byrnes seemed confident he had Roosevelt's backing, and that he had promised to nominate Byrnes.

At the convention in Chicago, meanwhile, knowing noth-ing about the Roosevelt letters or note, Truman kept his promise and worked hard for Byrnes.

He had breakfast with Sidney Hillman, a powerful labor leader, and asked him to support Byrnes. Hillman refused.

"We're for Wallace," said Hillman. He said they would also support William Douglas, however, and then he added, "There is only one other man we could consider supporting."

"Who?" asked Truman.

Hillman smiled. "I'm looking at him now."

CIO President Philip Murray said much the same thing for his labor organization, and William Green, head of the American Federation of Labor, was even more specific. "The AF of L is for you," he told Truman, "and will support no one else."

Truman told all these labor leaders that he was not a candidate, that he was for Byrnes, and he reported all these conversations back to Byrnes. Byrnes seemed unworried, still certain he had President Roosevelt's endorsement.

Hannegan now felt the time had come to show Truman the scribbled note of Roosevelt's, saying, "Bob, it's Truman. F.D.R."

"I don't believe the President wrote it," said Truman smiling. "I think you're just kidding me, Bob."

In nominating Truman for the vice-presidency, Senator Bennett Clark of Missouri, Truman's old political enemy, now said, ". . . Truman possesses the qualities of mind and heart to make a very splendid President in the event anything happens to Roosevelt."

Armed with the Roosevelt note and letters, Hannegan had lined up enough delegates to nominate Truman on the second ballot.

☆　　☆　　☆　　☆　　☆　　　　**8**

HARRY TRUMAN'S ACCEPTANCE SPEECH WAS one of the shortest on record, less than a hundred words, in which he noted that it was nine years and five months since he had first come to the Senate. "I don't know what else I can say except that I accept this great honor with all humility."

The crowds were so great that Mrs. Truman had difficulty pushing her way toward her husband. She asked him, "Are we going to have to go through this all the rest of our lives?" Later she told reporters, "I'm just getting excited," and when she was asked to describe her husband, she said, "He is the type of person who would be satisfied to eat beefsteak and fried potatoes every night."

Reporters also interviewed Truman's mother, who said, "I'm not a giggly woman, but I can't help smiling when people cheer at the mention of Harry's name." Then, thinking about it, she added that she wished her son could have remained a Senator where he "can do more good."

In their election campaign attacks on Truman, Republicans dredged up his past Pendergast association, his rumored membership in the Ku Klux Klan, his business failures, even the fact that he couldn't prevent the foreclosure of his mother's farm.

Truman absolutely denied any membership in the Klan, and told how bitterly they had fought him, even threatening his life. As for the Pendergast issue, he refused to dodge it. He freely admitted his friendship for Pendergast, insisted that Pendergast's word was his bond and that he had always kept his word to him. He added that politics needs leadership and Pendergast provided that necessary leadership when nobody else did. However, he did note that the Pendergast scandal happened several years after he himself had come to the Senate, and that the opposition had examined his record under political microscopes and found it completely honest.

He read most of his speeches, but occasionally he talked without notes, speaking his mind freely. These were almost always the speeches that listeners liked best. They had more humor, more obvious sincerity, more warmth. They were much more the mirror of the man himself.

The Republicans had picked New York Governor Thomas E. Dewey as their presidential candidate, and Governor of Ohio, John Bricker for Vice-President. Dewey charged that the Democratic administration had "grown old in office." Roosevelt charged that this was not the time to turn our government over to "inexperienced and immature hands."

Hannegan invited Truman to join a group of top party leaders at his rooms at the Blackstone Hotel. He and Truman sat on the bed while Hannegan put in a telephone call to President Roosevelt in San Diego.

Roosevelt had a habit of shouting into a telephone, and Hannegan held the receiver far from his ear so that Truman could also hear the conversation.

"Bob, have you got that fellow lined up yet?" yelled Roosevelt.

"No," said Hannegan, "he's the contrariest Missouri mule I've ever dealt with."

"Well," shouted Roosevelt, "you tell him if he wants to break up the Democratic party in the middle of the war, that's his responsibility."

Truman listened, almost unbelieving.

"I was, to put it mildly, stunned," Truman wrote later. But he told Hannegan, still hesitating, "Well, if he feels that way about it, I guess I'll have to take it."

Reporters afterward quoted Truman as saying, "I never ran for a political office I wanted. But I've fought for every one I ever had."

Byrnes withdrew from the race, but he was bitter when Truman called and told him what had happened.

Wallace, however, was determined to fight for the nomination. He still had strong support from the big cities, from labor and from a packed convention gallery.

When Truman met Roosevelt to discuss campaign plans, Roosevelt told him, "Travel by train; don't fly."

Truman asked him why.

"Because one of us has got to stay alive," said Roosevelt.

Truman traveled in a private railroad car named the Henry Stanley, which toured up and down and across the country. In a speech he made most often, Truman said, "This is no time for a change . . . you can't afford to take a chance. . . ."

Usually, after the day's stops and speeches, he would wander into the press car, wearing an old dressing gown and house slippers and say to the reporters, "How about it, boys? Let's have a little ten-cent ante." And the poker game would begin. Poker was Truman's safety valve. That and reading were his way of relaxing. He wasn't a real gambler because he wasn't interested in the money as much as in the game itself. He adjusted stakes according to the people with whom he played, and there was usually a limit on the amount anyone could lose, especially when he played with his staff.

He played poker the way he played politics. He didn't hesitate to take risks, and he played a hard-hitting game and seldom bluffed. He based his game more on an analysis of the other players than on the cards, and he found the poker table a good place to judge men.

During the campaign, he did everything from piano-playing to an Indian war dance, but he still found it "one of the easiest campaigns of them all."

For President Roosevelt it was not always easy. To prove to the American people that he was still physically fit, he insisted on riding through a pouring rain in New York City for some fifty miles. But he also had some fun during the campaign with his famous "Fala" speech, in which he said: "These Republican leaders have not been content with attacks upon me, my wife, or my sons—they now include my little dog Fala. Unlike the members of my family, he resents this. Being a Scottie, as soon as he learned that the Republican fiction writers had concocted a story that I had left him behind on an Aleutian island and had sent a destroyer back to find him at a cost to the taxpayers of two or three or twenty million dollars, his Scotch soul was furious. He has not been the same dog since."

Nobody laughed harder at that than Harry Truman. It was the kind of political humor he loved.

The nation's press had cautiously predicted a close election, but the Roosevelt-Truman victory was a smashing one.

Their popular vote was 25,602,504 to Dewey's 22,006,285. More spectacular was the final electoral vote: 432 to 99.

After their election victory, Truman said that he felt about being Vice-President a great deal like the farmer who said, "I have to go to town to get drunk and gosh, how I dread it!"

Somebody jokingly asked him what he planned to do with all the free time he would have as Vice-President.

"Study history," he said.

After the inauguration ceremony he called his mother in Missouri and asked if she had heard the ceremony on radio.

"Yes, I heard it all. Now you behave yourself up there, Harry. Now you behave yourself!"

And the Vice-President of the United States faithfully promised, "I will, Mamma."

Truman was Vice-President only six days when Tom Pendergast died. Instead of ignoring his death, as some political friends urged, Truman took an Army bomber to Kansas City to attend the funeral. "I'm sorry as I can be," Truman told reporters. "He was always my friend and I have always been his."

Even his enemies admired his courage.

Despite his high office, Vice-President Truman still maintained his five-room apartment on Connecticut Avenue, without a maid. Daughter Margaret was a student at Georgetown University, determined on a singing career, and they were a close-knit family with more social obligations than they wished.

Truman still maintained his old association with his Senate friends, opening his office to them in a way that Wallace never had. It was because of these friendships that he was able to persuade the Senate to confirm Henry Wallace as Secretary of Commerce in a very close vote. But the only time Truman voted was to break a tie and defeat an amendment that might have crippled our Lend Lease aid to our wartime allies.

Writing about Truman's new influence in the Senate, Roscoe Drummond said in the *Christian Science Monitor:* "Harry Truman is doing things for the vice-presidency. He is giving it new influence where influence counts most—in the Senate—helping to bring the President and Congress into a closer, more sympathetic working relationship."

But Truman's personal contact with the President was far from close. Except for the Cabinet meetings, Truman saw Roosevelt only twice. As for the Cabinet meetings, Roosevelt seldom discussed anything important there, and Cabinet members usually took up important problems with him after the meetings.

Tired and sick as he was, Roosevelt traveled to the Crimea to meet with Stalin and Churchill. At Yalta the three leaders of the world unsuccessfully tried to lay the foundations for a future peace. When he returned, the exhausted President addressed Congress while sitting down, and apologized for it.

Truman saw him briefly then, and was worried about his spent look. "I had a hollow feeling within me," he said later.

Not long before, Truman had gone walking with his old Army buddy from Battery D, Ed McKim. During their walk, McKim stopped in front of the White House and said, "Hey, bud, turn around and take a look. You're going to be living in that house before long."

Truman stared silently at the White House for a long time, then said, "Eddie, I'm afraid I am."

Vice-President Harry Truman was visiting his good friend Sam Rayburn, Speaker of the House of Representatives, when the phone rang. It was White House Press Secretary Steve Early, and he wanted to talk to Truman.

"Please come right over," Early told Truman in a strained voice, "and come in through the main Pennsylvania Avenue entrance."

Truman quickly headed for his office to get his hat, somehow slipping away from the three Secret Service men assigned to trail him. He reached the White House about 5:25 P.M. and was immediately taken to Mrs. Roosevelt's study on the second floor.

Mrs. Roosevelt, with her characteristic, graceful dignity, stepped forward and placed her arm gently around Truman's shoulder.

"Harry," she said quietly, "the President is dead."

Stunned into silence, Truman finally said, "Is there anything I can do for you?"

"Is there anything *we* can do for *you?*" replied Mrs. Roosevelt, "for you are the one in trouble now."

They brought the body of President Roosevelt from Warm Springs, Georgia, where he had died. Hundreds of thousands of grief-stricken people watched the train travel to Washington, carrying the body of the only President they had really known. He was a man who had come into leadership at a time of panic and crisis and charged them with a fresh faith. He had told them that "the only thing we have to fear is fear itself." Here was a President, of whom

Yank Magazine correspondent Debs Myers had said, "This crippled man had taken a crippled nation and helped it walk once more."

Harry Truman was stunned, but so was the nation—and so was the world. While Truman fought to control his tears, many millions of people throughout the world uncontrollably gave way to their grief.

At 7:09 P.M. on Thursday, April 12, 1945, Harry S. Truman became the thirty-third President of the United States.

Here was a man many had considered a failure at forty. While he had been a brave officer during World War I, he had failed as a farmer, as a storekeeper, as a businessman, and even in politics, for at the age of forty, he had been defeated for re-election as county judge after serving only a single term of office. And now, barely twenty years later, he was the President of the United States!

His wife Bess wept openly at his swearing-in ceremony, and the faces of the assembled Cabinet members were grim, their eyes wet.

"I, Harry S. Truman, do solemnly swear that I will faithfully execute the office of President of the United States, and will, to the best of my ability, preserve, protect, and defend the Constitution of the United States."

To the waiting newspapermen, Truman said, "Boys, if you ever pray, pray for me now. I don't know whether you fellows ever had a load of hay fall on you, but . . . I felt like the moon, the stars and all the planets had fallen on me. I've got the most terribly responsible job a man ever had."

"Good luck, Mr. President," said one of the reporters.

"I wish you didn't have to call me that," said Truman sadly and seriously.

After all, he had been Vice-President for only eighty-two days. Roosevelt had been away for most of that time, and he had hardly seen him. As a Senator, his complete concentration had been on the defense industries investigation. His knowledge of our progress and plans in the war and in the world had been minimal. He hadn't even been told that we had perfected something called an atomic bomb. He would have to absorb a massive amount of background knowledge on a huge variety of subjects in the shortest possible time.

There were many people in this country—and throughout the world—who did not think that Harry Truman could do it. They saw him as a friendly, bespectacled average American caught in a monumental position without the capacity to fill that job. Truman himself had his doubts.

But Mrs. Franklin D. Roosevelt once said, "There is something about the presidency that pulls out of a man the utmost of his potential."

Harry S. Truman was to become the living example of that remark.

Evaluating his new President and old friend, editor Roy Roberts of the Kansas City *Star* wrote:

Harry Truman is as far apart from both Roosevelt and Churchill as Hyde Park is from Independence. The new President is the average man. He started climbing the ladder in politics, with a political machine as his sponsor—the worst handicap to overcome in any possible climb to the Presidency. What a story in democracy, that a man approaching forty, and still looking at a horse as he plowed the corn rows, apparently not a success in life, just a little

117

less than twenty years ago, should find himself today President of the greatest and most powerful nation on earth.

Another Truman friend asked him, "Well, Harry, how are you going to behave, now that you are head of a nation?" Truman smiled and said, "Just as I did when I was a judge in Jackson County."

That meant a combination of toughness and good will, of cockiness and humility, a willingness to compromise on methods but seldom on principle, and a deep and abiding loyalty to all friends that would sometimes get him into trouble.

Roscoe Drummond suggested in the *Christian Science Monitor* that Truman had humility and self-confidence in equal proportions.

His humility springs from the fact that he recognizes that he is not an unusual man, that he is not outstandingly brilliant intellectually, nor possessed of a special genius of diplomacy. His self-confidence springs from the fact that he is profoundly aware of his role and responsibility, his authority and his weight as President of the United States.

Truman's first act as President of the United States was to reaffirm the American wish for a world organization, in the form of a United Nations, to help keep the peace. The preliminary meetings to set up the United Nations were scheduled to be held in San Francisco on April 2, and Truman announced that there would be no change in the arrangements.

The plan for this new world organization, to replace the

old League of Nations, had long been discussed by President Roosevelt and the five major powers, and finally settled at the previous Yalta Conference. Roosevelt already had selected the American delegation, headed by Secretary of State Edward Stettinius, and including leading Republican and Democratic Senators and Representatives.

While he himself was unable to attend the meeting in San Francisco, Truman made plain to our delegation that he believed in Woodrow Wilson's policy of self-determination for all countries, that he was against any form of colonialism anywhere.

Addressing a joint session of Congress the day after he became President, Truman said, "It is with a heavy heart that I stand before you, my friends and colleagues. . . . Tragic fate has thrust upon us grave responsibilities. We must carry on. Our departed leader never looked backward. He looked forward and moved forward. That is what he would want us to do. This is what America *will* do."

Truman's mother expressed the feelings of millions of Americans when she said: "I can't really be glad Harry's President because I am sorry President Roosevelt is dead. If he had been voted in, I'd be out waving a flag. But it does not seem right to be very happy, or wave any flags now."

Harry Truman was the seventh Vice-President to become President because of his predecessor's death.

Only twenty-four hours before, as Vice-President, he had presided over his last session of the Senate. The main discussion of that meeting concerned a water treaty between the United States and Mexico. After that session ended, he had walked down from the rostrum to the Senate floor,

119

patted his old desk gently, then told a reporter that he would rather be at that desk than at any other in the world.

Now as President of the United States, instead of water treaties, he had to worry about a world war that was still going on, and about the world peace that must follow. Instead of a single job behind a single desk, he now had six jobs in one—Chief Executive, maker of foreign policy, Commander-in-Chief, head of state, director of the legislative program, and leader of a political party.

The small boy whose mother had given him his prized set of "Great Men and Famous Women" had read all about Alexander the Great and Genghis Khan and Napoleon. But now that he was President, he knew that none of these great men of the past had as much power as the President of the United States.

He later said that being President was like riding a tiger, that a man had to keep on riding or else be swallowed.

A President of the United States never has time to stop, because there is always still another decision ahead that he has to make. Truman said he saw no point in looking back at past decisions, that if you make a mistake in one of those decisions, you simply correct it with another decision, and go ahead.

Truman believed in doing all his worrying before he made up his mind, never afterward. Once he made a decision, he forgot it and went to work on something else. That's probably one of the reasons why he never had any trouble sleeping at night.

To help him make the best decision, he surrounded himself with experts on the different problems of government. At first, Truman kept the Roosevelt Cabinet intact, but gradually he replaced them with his own people: Robert

Hannegan, as Postmaster General; Tom Clark, as Attorney General, Lewis Schwellenbach, as Secretary of Labor; Clinton Anderson, as Secretary of Agriculture; James Byrnes, as Secretary of State. These were not only his friends, but men whose judgment he trusted, men whom he felt he could depend on for facts.

"He wanted all the facts he could gather before he made up his mind," said Clark Clifford, one of his closest advisers. "But if he could get only eighty percent of the facts in the time available, he didn't let the missing twenty percent tie him up in indecision. He believed that even a wrong decision was better than no decision at all."

One of the first things he put on the wall of his White House office was a framed fragment of Mark Twain's handwriting that he found some fifteen years before. It read, "Always do right. This will gratify some people and astonish the rest."

And on his desk he put the sign: "THE BUCK STOPS HERE."

He also brought in a statuette of one of the two Presidents who meant most to him, Andrew Jackson. (The other was Thomas Jefferson.) And he put his small collection of historic pistols where he could see them.

He once told a radio official that his greatest handicap was "living the lives of two men—that of President and that of a human being."

Truman, the human being, could write this letter to his mother and sister in Grandview, Missouri:

Dear Mama and Mary:

I am sixty-one this morning, and I slept in the President's room in the White House last night. They have finished the painting and have some of the furniture in place. I'm hoping it will all be ready for you by Friday. My expensive gold pen doesn't work as well as it should.

This will be an historical day. At nine o'clock this morning I must make a broadcast to the country: announcing the German surrender. The papers were signed yesterday morning and hostilities will cease on all fronts at midnight tonight. Isn't that some birthday present? . . .

Truman, the human being, worried about Margaret's piano that had to be hoisted through a second-story window.

Truman, the human being, laughed when Mrs. Roosevelt's grandson searched through one of the closets for something he had left behind, and said, "Her closets are as messy as Grandma's."

Truman, the human being, could say, "I am always so lonesome when the family leaves. I have no one to raise a fuss over my neckties and my haircuts."

Truman, the human being, could amaze the White House servants at a family dinner by flipping a watermelon seed at his wife, duck when she flipped one back and then start a battle of flipping watermelon seeds, even hitting the White House butler.

His wife refused to hold regular press conferences, tried to keep completely out of the limelight. Maybe her husband was public property, she said, "but I'm not."

"You don't have to know me," she said. "Know Harry, he's the President. I'm only his wife and the mother of his daughter, and that's what I intend to remain."

It was only forty-seven blocks from their third-floor apartment on Connecticut Avenue to the White House, but it was the difference between a home and a goldfish bowl.

Instead of having her husband regularly dry the dishes, she now had thirty-one servants. Instead of small family parties at the piano, she now had to worry about impressive state dinners and fancy foreign receptions. And how would their twenty-year-old daughter be changed by all this? And how would it change her husband?

It didn't seem to change him too much. He still woke up every morning close to six o'clock, shaved himself with a safety razor, wore the same neat, quiet suits with the American Legion button in his lapel, ate the same breakfast of juice, cereal (hot in winter, dry otherwise), two pieces of whole wheat toast and a glass of milk, the same breakfast he ate throughout his life—and he never drank coffee.

And he always managed his morning walk, at a brisk military pace.

It was true that the important people of the world now waited to see him, talk to him, write to him. It was true that anything he said now had headline value. It was true that he was now one of the most important men in the world.

"To keep from going high hat and stuffed shirt," he wrote his mother and sister, "I have to keep in mind Luke 6:26." (This passage read: "Woe unto you, when all men shall speak well of you! for so did their fathers to the false prophets.") And then he added: "How would you like to be President of the *Etats-Unis*? It's a hell of a life. . . ."

His mother arrived in Washington on the presidential plane. She was then ninety-two, and when she saw the waiting reporters, she said, "Oh, fiddlesticks. If I'd known this, I wouldn't have come." She still had her Confederate sympathies and had said to her other son, Vivian, "You tell

Harry, if he puts me in the room with Lincoln's bed in it, I'll sleep on the floor."

When Truman introduced her to one of his friends, saying, "Mama, this is George Allen, a Democrat from Mississippi. He says he never saw a Republican until he was twelve years old," she had a quick response: "He didn't miss much."

"She was just the same Mama she had always been," said Truman afterward.

☆　　☆　　☆　　☆　　☆　　9

WHILE THE WAR IN EUROPE ENDED, OUR FIGHT against the Japanese in the Pacific looked like a long war. The Japanese were inflicting heavy damage on our Navy with their so-called suicide kamikaze pilots. These pilots flew their planes and bombs directly onto a target ship, knowing in advance that the exploding crash would cost their lives. It seemed more and more likely, even though we were slowly pushing them back, that the Japanese would refuse to surrender until we had invaded Japan itself and defeated them there.

So on the one hand, Truman had to contend with war; on the other hand, he had to plan for the peace.

With Hitler dead and Germany defeated, the two strong men in Europe were England's Churchill and Russia's Stalin. Even though both these men faced the huge task of the reconstruction of their battered countries, and even though both countries had suffered enormous casualties in dead and wounded, Churchill and Stalin still played the see-saw game of controlling the political power of Europe.

Truman finally felt that the time had come to meet with these two leaders, as President Roosevelt had done.

125

He wrote to his mother about his plans to meet Churchill and Stalin at Potsdam in Germany for a summit meeting, and what a chore it was to take his tuxedo, tails and "preacher hat, high hat, low hat, hard hat." He told her how he had his briefcase all filled up with information on past conferences and suggestions on what he should do and say, and that he wished he didn't have to go, but he had to.

Truman liked Churchill, argued with him about many things but never seriously disagreed with him. He regarded Churchill as a hard bargainer who liked to argue about everything, but always finally found him on the right side.

Truman got along well with Stalin, too, found him pleasant to talk to, compared him favorably to Tom Pendergast and even saw similarities between the political situation in Russia and Jackson County, Missouri. The two men also shared a mutual appreciation of Chopin's music. During a piano concert by an American Army sergeant, Eugene List, President Truman even volunteered to turn the pages of the music.

After a Stalin state dinner, Truman wrote his mother about the menu that started with caviar and vodka and ended with watermelon and champagne, with smoked fish, fresh fish, venison, chicken, duck and all sorts of vegetables in between. Truman wrote that it also seemed to include a toast to somebody every five minutes. He ended the letter with the words, "It was a wow!"

One Truman habit that didn't seem to fit into the summit meeting was the fact that he was an early riser—while Stalin and Churchill both woke late and worked late. This made Truman's days extra long. In addition, there was always the steady stream of papers arriving from Washington.

A President of the United States takes his office with him wherever he goes.

The Potsdam Conference of July, 1945, also known as the Berlin Conference, was the last summit meeting of the war. In the thirteen sessions that lasted two weeks, the three big powers set down the terms for a conquered Germany. They decided on complete disarmament and demilitarization, insisted that the Nazi leaders involved in atrocities and war crimes must be brought to justice. The communique said: "It is not the intention of the Allies to destroy or enslave the German people. It is the intention of the Allies that the German people be given the opportunity to prepare for the eventual reconstruction of their life on a democratic and peaceful basis . . . take their place among the free and peaceful peoples of the world."

The conference also decided on the amount of reparations each country should get from Germany, returned the territories of other countries that Hitler had taken, and put into immediate effect the previous Yalta Conference agreement that divided Germany into four separate zones of occupation: American, British, French and Russian.

Truman had hoped to settle many other controversial issues, among them the need for free elections in Poland, but he never got around to them because all three major powers wanted to talk about different things. There was the added difficulty of talking to Stalin through an interpreter, and Truman often found himself in the middle of stormy sessions acting as a kind of mediator between Churchill and Stalin. As Secretary of State Byrnes described it, "The United States has unfortunately found that if it agrees with the Soviet delegation, the British delegation does not agree, and if it agrees with the British, then the Soviet disagrees."

The long sessions irritated Truman because there seemed to be more words than action. He told the others that he hadn't come simply to discuss; he came to decide.

Complicating the conference was a British national election and Churchill had to go home and face the voters. In a surprise result, the voters replaced their wartime Prime Minister with a Labor government headed by Clement Attlee. Since Attlee had served as Churchill's Deputy Prime Minister and had attended all the sessions of the conference, he was able to continue where Churchill had left off. Churchill did not return with Attlee to finish the conference.

"Well, another week has gone," Truman wrote his mother, "and I'm still in this Godforsaken country awaiting the return of the new British Prime Minister."

"You never saw such a pigheaded people as the Russians," wrote Truman in another letter. "I hope I never have to hold another conference with them."

He inspected American troops in Germany before he left, and told them, "I hope when you come home you will find home as you want it."

But something had happened while Truman was at Potsdam that would change the meaning of all the homes in the world. Truman had received word that the first atomic bomb had been successfully tested. He had never even known about this bomb until he became President—now it was his decision on whether or not it should be used in the war against Japan.

Back at his office in the White House, the sign said: "THE BUCK STOPS HERE." He could collect all the facts, all the opinions from everyone and everywhere, but the final, lonely decision was his.

He knew what it meant. He knew that this single bomb would kill and cripple tens of thousands of people, many of them women and children. He knew that this single bomb could smash a city into an unrecognizable trash heap. And he knew that this single successful atomic bomb would introduce a new war horror into the world.

He knew all this, and yet he saw something else. Our troops were expecting to invade Japan in a very short time. Our generals had estimated that it would take 1,500,000 men to make that invasion and that perhaps 500,000 would be casualties and 250,000 of them might be killed. As President of the United States, he felt it his sworn duty to save the lives of those Americans, and use this weapon of war to end the war quickly.

"I did not hesitate to order the use of the bomb on military targets," Truman later said. "I wanted to save half a million boys on our side and as many on the other side. I never lost any sleep over my decision."

All his top military advisers agreed. There had been some discussion of a demonstration of the bomb, before its actual use, so that the Japanese could see its horror, and surrender. But his scientific advisers told Truman that such a demonstration was not advisable. Truman told Stalin about the new atomic bomb, and Stalin's reaction was simply that he hoped the Americans would make "good use of it against the Japanese."

Truman first asked the Japanese to surrender, and our planes dropped around 27,000,000 leaflets passing this message on to the Japanese people. But the Japanese government called our ultimatum "absurd," and refused. Then Truman had Secretary of War Henry Stimson present his list of suggested military targets. Of the four selected cities, Truman approved the use of the A-bomb on any two of them.

A single plane dropped the single atomic bomb on Hiroshima in Japan on August 6 at 8:15 A.M., and a city of 343,000 people seemed to vanish into a mushroom. Among the rubble were almost 100,000 people killed or missing. "Look at the blood on our hands," a scientist told Truman months later.

Truman told him simply, "Your job is to invent; my job is to decide what use shall be made of the invention. I did what I believed needed to be done, what I felt had to be done."

The Japanese refused to surrender after Hiroshima, even after Truman broadcast warning of further destruction. Three days later, Truman ordered another atomic bomb dropped, this one on Nagasaki. The Russians had also declared war on Japan the day before. Japan surrendered. The war was over.

The United States wanted neither territory nor reparations, Truman said. "Maybe the teachings of the Sermon on the Mount could be put into effect," he later wrote.

More than ever before, Truman felt the urgent need for a strong United Nations. Speaking before the Senate, he had asked and received quick American approval of the United Nations Charter. He had said:

The objectives of this charter are clear:
It seeks to prevent future wars.

130

It seeks to settle international disputes by peaceful means, in conformity with the principles of justice.

It seeks to promote world-wide progress and better standards of living.

It seeks to achieve universal respect for—and observance of—human rights and fundamental freedoms for all men and women—without distinction as to race, language or religion.

It also sought to fulfill a prophecy in a poem called "Locksley Hall," which Harry Truman had carried in his wallet since he was ten years old, in which the final two lines were:

"Till the war drums throb no longer and the battle flags were furled In the parliament of man, the federation of the world."

After the war was over, a reporter remembered Truman saying simply, "We can go the wrong way now and spoil the whole thing."

"The one ambition that I have," he told a Texas audience, "is to see a peaceful, happy world. If that can't be accomplished, there is nothing else worthwhile."

"If we had this charter a few years ago," he said in another speech, "and above all the will to use it—millions now dead would be alive. If we should falter in the future in our will to use it, millions now living will surely die."

The horror of the atomic bomb was much on his mind. "No one can foresee what another war would mean to our cities and our own people," he said.

"Ever since Hiroshima I had never stopped thinking about the frightful implications of the atomic bomb," he later wrote. "We knew that this revolutionary scientific creation could destroy civilization unless put under control and placed at the service of mankind."

As a beginning, he set up the Atomic Energy Commission and started immediate discussion with our allies on an international policy on atomic control.

Now Truman was faced with the postwar problems of peace, the problems of more than twelve million returning war veterans, the problems of a national reconversion of men and industry. His was a program aimed at that American soldier in Germany to whom he had said, *"I hope when you come home, you'll find home as you want it."*

Truman sent Congress a twenty-one-point program which covered everything from Social Security to civil rights, from minimum wages to farm price supports, from unemployment compensation to public housing, from aid to education to a program of national health. The date was September 6, 1945, "the date that symbolizes for me my assumption of the office of President in my own right," wrote Truman. "It was on that day and with this message that I first spelled out the details of the program of liberalism and progressivism which was to be the foundation of my administration." It was later known as the Fair Deal.

"Not even President Roosevelt ever asked for so much at one sitting," said Republican Congressional leader Joseph Martin. "It is just a case of outdealing the New Deal."

Truman had some answers and reasons. He wanted to "put human welfare first and profit second." And elsewhere he added, "I don't believe in goverment for special privilege! Our resources should be used for the benefit of all the people." Then he repeated again and again, "Representatives are elected by districts. They all have local interests which they're supposed to represent in Congress. That's the reason it's set up that way. But the President is elected by the whole people and he must look out for the interests of all the people. There are about fifteen million people in the country who can afford to have a representative in Washington to look after their interests in addition to the Congressmen and Senators that they have there, and they're called lobbyists. There's nothing wrong with them. They have a perfect right to do that, but there are one hundred and fifty million people who can't afford that. They have but one man in the government to look after their interests, and that's the President of the United States. He is the lobbyist for one hundred and fifty million people, for all the people of America."

He felt this deeply. He remembered the faces of a depressed and defeated American people during the early 1930's when he was a county judge crisscrossing the country. He remembered the strong faith of the many Americans— and the greed of a few—when he traveled the country again just before the start of World War II. Above all, always fresh in his mind were the faces and faith of his friends and neighbors in Jackson County, Missouri. If he was an "average American" as they were, then Harry Truman was proud of it, and said so.

But the American newspapers now used this "average American" phrase as a point of attack and ridicule. After President Roosevelt's death, most of the American newspapers were properly patriotic in their promised support of unity behind the new President. The war was still going on, and such support seemed necessary. Their mood was, "I'm just wild about Harry." With the war over, however, the press and the people returned to politics, as usual, and the newspaper mood was, "I'm just *mild* about Harry."

After all, this was not unexpected. The majority of American newspapers have been politically Republican, and were bitterly critical of President Roosevelt and his New Deal throughout his three terms. For them, the Truman Fair Deal seemed a strong echo of the New Deal. As for the American people, it was unrealistic to expect the wartime unity of feeling and purpose to last long.

The same sort of expected split took place in Congress. With the war over, Congress again voted on party lines and sectional feelings. Southern Democrats joined with Republicans to vote against any Civil Rights issues. Conservatives of both parties grouped together, as they had during the Roosevelt administrations, to vote against the more liberal Fair Deal proposals. Despite his personal friendships with many members of Congress, Truman saw little of his Fair Deal enacted into law.

There was something else that cost Truman considerable popularity with the American people: his deep loyalty to his friends. He had brought many of his Missouri friends to Washington and found jobs for them, including some of his old Army buddies such as Harry Vaughan. He made Vaughan his military aide because he felt he needed somebody close with whom he could relax. Vaughan made the mistake of accepting gifts from people who presumably wanted his friendship and influence. Other of Truman's Missouri friends accepted a variety of gifts, including mink coats.

Newspapers saw in such gifts a strong hint of political corruption and headlined these facts across the country.

134

Instead of keeping politically quiet about all this, Truman heatedly defended all his friends. This only aggravated the irritation of the press and the people. Comedians and columnist kept the issue alive with a whole series of jokes, but they were bitter jokes.

But back home in Missouri, however, he was still much loved. On his first trip home, the turnout was overwhelming. "All these people have seen me two or three times a day for the last thirty or forty years," Truman said. "I can't see what there is about me now that would make them turn out like they did today."

They gave him an honorary degree at the Kansas City School of Law, where he had been a night student for two and a half years. But it was at the county fair at Caruthersville, Missouri, that he made his report to his people. After outlining everything he had done during his presidency of six months, he said, "We are going to have difficulties. We can't do anything worthwhile without difficulties. No man who ever accomplished anything can expect to do it without making mistakes. The man who never does anything never makes any mistakes."

The difficulties soon began to multiply. When the railroad unions threatened to strike, Truman called their leaders to the White House and told them, "If you think I'm going to sit here and let you tie up this country, you're crazy. I am going to protect the public and we are going to run these railroads and you can put that in your pipe and smoke it!"

Truman then prepared a speech asking Congress to draft any striking workers into the Army and put them back running the trains as American soldiers. In his speech, he said, "What we are dealing with here is not labor as a whole. We are dealing with a handful of men who are striking against their own government and against every one of their fellow citizens."

Soon afterward, while Truman was still speaking, somebody handed him a note, which he read and then announced to the cheering Senate, "Word has just been received that the railroad strike has been settled on terms proposed by the President!"

Truman also had a showdown fight with John L. Lewis, head of the United Mine Workers who had called on his four hundred thousand members to strike. Truman felt that a country without coal would be crippled just as badly as a country without railroads. He ordered his Attorney General to get a federal court order to cancel the strike. Lewis defied the injunction and a federal court fined him and his union more than three and a half million dollars, which the Supreme Court later cut to seven hundred thousand. But it stopped the strike.

The CIO then called Truman the country's Number One strikebreaker, and John L. Lewis bitterly described him as ". . . totally unfitted for the position . . . he is a malignant, scheming sort of an individual who is dangerous not only to the United Mine Workers, but dangerous to the United States of America."

Truman seemed to have lost his labor support.

His troubles soon became international. He had created a world-wide tempest when he invited Winston Churchill to make a speech at Westminister, a small Missouri college. In it, Churchill had said, ". . . From Stettin in the Baltic to

136

Trieste in the Adriatic, an iron curtain has descended across the continent."

The phrase "iron curtain" caught the imagination of the world. In that speech, Churchill asked that the United States lead an anti-Communist bloc of nations to prevent the expansion of the Soviet Union into the small countries of eastern Europe.

But President Truman felt that he must direct the American foreign policy as carefully as he did at Potsdam.

Truman's Secretary of State at that time was James Byrnes, the same man whom he had once agreed to nominate for the vice-presidency in 1944. Now he fired him because he felt that Byrnes compromised with the Russians too much, against his expressed wishes and without informing him.

Specifically, Byrnes had agreed to a five-year United States–Russian trusteeship in Korea, instead of calling for an election of a unified Korean government. Byrnes also had agreed to include Russia in a Far Eastern Commission to rehabilitate Japan, and Truman felt they had no right to be on that commission, since they had entered the war at the very tail end. Finally, Byrnes also had agreed to a Paris Conference the following year to discuss subjects that Russia wanted to discuss—and Truman didn't. In a sum-up letter, which he read aloud to Byrnes, Truman said, "I'm tired of babying the Soviets."

The humility Truman originally had for the presidency now disappeared. He had become increasingly aware of the responsibility and power of that office. As President of the United States, it was he who made its foreign policy, he who gave the orders to his Cabinet and his government officials, and he could not have people in important positions who were not in agreement with his policies.

For those reasons, he also fired Henry Wallace as Secretary of Commerce, since one of his speeches had directly attacked the Truman foreign policy toward Russia.

Truman's popularity dropped to a new low during the fall of 1946. The Republican party in the Congressional elections that year used a simple two-word slogan, "Had enough?" In that election, Republicans won control of both the House of Representatives and the Senate.

Truman's military aide and friend, General Vaughan, said of the President, "If I can give him a belly laugh a day, I think I have earned my pay."

At one low point, Truman's press secretary, Charlie Ross, who had known him since high school, said that Truman would rather be right than President. Commenting on that in the privacy of a letter to his mother, Truman said that he would rather be anything than President.

A major part of the presidential problems was the constant ebb and flow of tension between this country and Soviet Russia. This tension took a new twist in the Middle East, when Russia began putting increased pressure on Iran, a small country that faced her frontier. During World War II she had stationed her troops in northern Iran, while the Americans and British had their troops in the southern part of the country. At a postwar conference in London, it was agreed that all countries should withdraw their troops from Iran. However, Truman received intelligence reports that the Soviets were sending more Russian troops to northern Iran, stirring up a movement for that province to declare its independence from the rest of the country and thereby move it closer to Communist control.

In a private note to Stalin, Truman warned that he was ordering our Mediterranean fleet into the Persian Gulf, and then warned him to remove his Soviet troops from Iran before our Navy arrived. Stalin quickly complied. Our military strength—including our possession of the atomic bomb which the Russians did not yet have—was strong enough to earn Stalin's extreme respect, especially in face of a direct threat.

After World War II, the United States had emerged as the leading power of the world. Communist Russia had become its strongest rival. Battered badly by the war, Great Britain had made the slowest recovery and no longer could maintain its original status as a world power.

Great Britain felt economically unable to maintain her military aid to Greece and Turkey, and a British withdrawal meant that both countries would probably fall under Communist control. Truman decided to move into those countries with American aid. He did this against the better judgment of many prominent Americans who felt we were overcommitting ourselves. But Truman felt no hesitation in his action. In fact, in the first draft of his speech to Congress, the key sentence read, "I believe that it should be the policy of the United States . . ."

"I took my pencil," said Truman, "scratched out 'should' and wrote in 'must.'" In several other places, he did the same thing. He wanted no hedging in this speech. This was America's answer to the surge of expansion of Communist tyranny. It had to be clear and free of hesitation or double talk.

The sentence finally read, "I believe that it must be the policy of the United States to support free people who are resisting attempted subjugation by armed minorities or by outside pressures. I believe we must assist free peoples to work out their own destinies in their own way. . . ."

Not only were Greece and Turkey saved from Communism by this so-called Truman Doctrine, but out of it grew the Marshall Plan. The Marshall Plan was actually born in a speech Truman was scheduled to make at Teacher's College in Cleveland, Mississippi. His mother was seriously ill, and he felt it necessary to visit her, and so he asked Undersecretary of State Dean Acheson to read his speech for him. The speech urged that the United States push ahead with the reconstruction of the great workshops of Europe. . . . The war will not be over until the people of the world can again feed and clothe themselves and face the future with some degree of confidence. . . ."

Later, General George Marshall, who replaced Byrnes as Secretary of State, expanded on Truman's idea in a commencement speech at Harvard. It grew into a plan that called for seventeen billion dollars' worth of aid to be distributed in four years. Most historians now generally agree that it was the Marshall Plan that saved the faltering free countries of Europe from communism.

This Marshall Plan was based on much more than a matter of money—it was a major plan to help Europe help itself. It asked European countries to figure out their own problems and their own needs, and arrive at solutions together. In that way, Truman felt, Europe could agree on a cooperative plan to use the full productive resources of the whole continent for *all* their countries. Before then, each country was busily concerned with its own problems and its own piecemeal solutions. The Marshall Plan put the whole program on a huge scale of mutual cooperation, with the United States supplying money, equipment, technical help.

Instead of being a program of American charity and handout, it became a program of European reconstruction and hope.

Of the whole Truman administration record, this was certainly one of his most important acts.

Truman's mother died at the age of ninety-four, while his plane was still in the air, en route to Grandview. One of the last things she had asked him concerned the upcoming 1948 election.

"Harry, are you going to run?" she asked.

"I don't know, Mama."

Her voice then sounded impatient. "Don't you think it's about time you made up your mind?"

She was right.

☆　☆　☆　☆　☆　　**10**

WHY WOULD ANYONE WANT TO BE PRESIDENT of the United States? The prestige, the power? Of course. That, plus the enormous satisfaction of accomplishment. And Harry Truman had a strong sense of history.

But there are some aspects that hurt deeply: The frustration of seeing a completely prepared program of action go down the drain because of Congressional disapproval; the intense bitterness of a political opposition that often hit hard at your family and your friends; a growing disapproval by the American public and the press.

All these things had happened to Harry Truman during his first term in office. Bess Truman felt them all, and plainly didn't want her husband to run for re-election in 1948. She told a reporter, "I don't want my husband renominated if it will interfere with our family life. My family is the most important thing to me."

It was similarly important to Harry Truman. He constantly consulted his wife on all kinds of controversial subjects that came up. And whenever he did something that his wife thought was wrong, she let him know what she thought. Her influence on him was important.

But this was more than a personal decision. He had an

obligation to the programs he had proposed, programs he had started—everything from civil rights to the Marshall Plan. He wanted the fight for these programs continued because he felt them vital to the future of the country and the future of peace in our world. He felt an obligation to his political party. He believed he had a better chance to win than any other Democratic candidate, despite the Gallup poll which showed his popularity dropping from 70 percent to 36 percent. He felt an obligation to his friends and associates who had believed so strongly in what he was doing, and who depended on him to follow through and prove he was right.

And, somewhere deep inside him, he felt this quiet obligation to the memory of his mother. More than anything else, she had wanted him to be elected, on his own merit, as President of the United States.

For all these reasons, Truman decided to run again.

The odds seemed tremendous.

When he delivered his State of the Union message to the second session of the Eightieth Congress at the beginning of 1948, the New York *Times* reported its reception as "extraordinarily chilly." In it, he reiterated his requests for new laws for public housing, aid to education, increased civil rights legislation including a Fair Employment Practices Act, as well as a tax cut of forty dollars for every taxpayer. The only time Congress really applauded during that speech was after Truman's statement that he would enforce the Taft-Hartley Act.

Truman later called the Eightieth Congress the "worst Congress" (he had earlier given that title to the Seventy-ninth Congress), mainly because they passed almost none of his requested major domestic legislation. Not only did it refuse to spend money on public housing or education, and more legal civil rights guarantees, but it also turned down his request for a national health bill, expanded Social Security, increased funds for soil conservation.

The only major law they did pass was the one he did not want—the Taft-Hartley Labor Act. Truman had asked Congress for a bill to strengthen the Department of Labor in handling labor-management relations and ending jurisdictional strikes. Instead, Congress passed this Taft-Hartley law which outlawed industry-wide strikes, mass picketing, and a number of other things which deeply antagonized labor. Many liberals felt that this law was aimed solely at labor, instead of trying to correct the main abuses of both labor *and* management.

Truman vetoed that law, but it was passed over his veto. It was, however, a strong political issue in the campaign which had already started. Most of the press now hit Truman hard.

Time Magazine described him as "awkward, uninspired, and, above all, mediocre."

Truman hit back the next month, describing Republicans as a "bunch of reactionaries who are trying to turn us back to 1896," and he added, "These men who live in the past remind me of a toy I'm sure you've all seen. The toy is a small wooden bird called the 'floogie bird.' Around the floogie bird's neck is a label reading, 'I fly backward. I don't care where I'm going. I just want to see where I've been."

But the key fact was that the strongest opposition to Truman at that time didn't come from Republicans; it came from Democrats. The Democratic party was a combination of the conservative South, organized labor, big-city political machines, as well as a fusion of assorted minority groups. Somehow Truman had managed to antagonize strong sections of all of them. The cartoon Truman then liked best had appeared in the Washington *Star* and showed him being approached by a goggle-eyed woman who says, "You mean you'd rather be right than President?"

Truman had lost much of the party's liberal support when he fired Henry Wallace, the last Roosevelt New Dealer in his Cabinet. Wallace later announced himself as the presidential nominee of the newly formed Progressive party. *The New Republic* Magazine predicted that Wallace would pull twenty million votes, and even such an astute political observer as James Farley, F.D.R.'s campaign manager, felt that Wallace could get some six million votes. In either case, it could seriously cripple the Truman candidacy.

Truman's relations with labor leaders were also poor. True, they felt he had shown courage in his veto of the Taft-Hartley Act. This was an act which most labor leaders felt limited their right to strike and interfered with their right of collective bargaining with management. They called it "a slave labor bill," and Congress passed it over Truman's veto. But these same labor leaders felt that Truman was guilty of government strikebreaking with his threat to draft railroad workers into the Army during a strike crisis. Daniel Tobin of the Teamsters' Union afterward said of Truman: "That squeaky-voiced tinhorn ... I want nothing to do with him."

Neither did the South seem to want him any more. Congressman Eugene Cox of Georgia said, "Harlem is wielding more influence with the Administration than the entire white South." Cox was referring to the Truman message to Congress asking for a permanent Commission on Civil Rights, as well as laws protecting the Negro's right to vote, laws outlawing lynching, the poll tax and segregation in interstate commerce. It also recommended a permanent Federal Employment Practices Division to prevent discrimination in job employment. The Baltimore *Afro-American* called it "one of the most significant documents of all time," but southern Senators called it "a lynching of the Constitution." Senator Eastland of Mississippi sharply warned, "By withholding the electoral votes, the South can defeat in 1948 any Democratic candidate."

It hardly seemed possible that this President, who had angered so many of the most powerful political groups in the country, could have any real hope of winning either the nomination or the election.

Governor Laney of Arkansas stuck the knife in a little deeper when he said, "We don't want to run a race with a dead Missouri mule."

One newspaper now regularly referred to the President as *"Thruman."* And even his best friends repeatedly urged him not to run. But back in Missouri in 1940, when it looked as though he were a hopeless candidate for re-election to the Senate, his best friends had similarly urged him not to run.

Truman wrote about that to a Missouri dentist from Salisbury, who had described himself as a lifelong Democrat. This dentist Democrat had urged Truman, "Regardless of the justice or the injustice, I believe that both popular opinion and opinions of liberals everywhere is that new leadership of the party is essential to victory this year."

Truman answered, ". . . I was not brought up to run from a fight.

"A great many of you Democrats in 1940 ran off after a

147

certain governor (Stark) who was trying to cut my throat, and he didn't do it successfully—nothing is going to stop me this time."

Then Truman officially announced his candidacy. He felt he still had a mission to perform, he said, "to bring about world peace."

Republican Chairman Reece commented that the Truman announcement of his candidacy hit "with the terrific impact of a poached egg on a feather bed."

But something else had been brewing that seemed to have considerably more impact. A group of leading Democrats decided to draft General Dwight D. Eisenhower as their presidential candidate. Eisenhower already had answered a similar Republican offer, saying, "I could not accept the nomination even under the remote circumstance that it would be tendered me. . . . The necessary and wise subordination of the military to civil power will be best sustained when lifelong professional soldiers abstain from seeking high political office."

But this didn't stop the Democratic draft. Such a combination of leaders as Franklin D. Roosevelt, Jr., Senator Richard Russell, Philip Murray of the CIO, Chicago political boss Jack Arvey, Mayor Hubert Humphrey of Minneapolis, Boss Frank Hague of Jersey City all announced for Eisenhower. They claimed at least one hundred and fifty electoral votes.

Truman seemed unworried. Back at the Potsdam Conference he had met General Eisenhower, and Eisenhower reported their conversation in his book *Crusade in Europe*.

"General, there is nothing you may want that I won't try to help you get," Truman had said. "That definitely and specifically includes the presidency in 1948."

"Mr. President," Eisenhower answered smiling, "I don't know who will be your opponent for the presidency, but it will not be I."

But even if Eisenhower had changed his mind, Truman still felt confident of the Democratic nomination.

"In 1948 I was able to control the nomination," he later wrote. "Presidential control of the convention is a political principle which has not been violated in political history. The President is traditionally the leader of his party. He has great influence with the National Committee, and usually the party will nominate a chairman of the convention who is friendly to the President, and the chairman controls the organization of the convention. The convention will operate in the manner in which the chairman and the President want it to."

Truman might also have added that the President controls party patronage, deciding the flow of political jobs, and this gives him a specific control over most delegates. There was also a psychological factor: for a party to repudiate its President meant repudiation of the record of the party.

"When I had made up my mind to run," Truman wrote, "those in the party who turned against me could do nothing to prevent it."

As if to prove that, a meeting of midwestern delegates in April ignored the Eisenhower boom, and pledged 156 delegate votes for Truman. With the Democratic National Convention scheduled for July 12, Truman forces picked up 423 pledged votes by early May.

But Truman decided to find out for himself how the American people felt. Invited to accept an honorary degree at the University of California, he turned the trip into a train tour through eighteen strategic states, with five major scheduled speeches. He smilingly referred to it as a "non-political trip" and said, "If I felt any better, I couldn't stand it."

It was a whistle-stop tour, with a speech at every stop, and there were seventy-six of them. The more he talked, the tougher he got, and he kept his focus on the Eightieth Congress which he had described as "the worst Congress you've ever had." At Grand Island, Nebraska, they gave him a pair of cowboy spurs and he told the crowd, "When I get them on, I can take Congress to town." When somebody else gave him a pair of cowboy boots, he said, "I really can take Congress for a ride now."

Before his trip he had written in his diary on May 6, "I may have to become an 'orator.' I heard a definition of an orator once—'He is an honest man who can communicate his views and make others believe he is right.' Wish I could do that."

But again, he did much better in his folksy off-the-cuff speeches than in his orations. In Idaho, he told the potato-prowd people of the soldier he met in Maine who refused to peel potatoes because they were from Maine and not Idaho; in California, he praised their sunshine. "This is the real thing. It makes Florida look like thirty cents." In Omaha, Nebraska, he said, "I was in business during the depression of the twenties, and you all know what happened to me."

And in Winslow, Arizona, he said that the country's greatest epitaph was in Tombstone, Arizona: "Here lies Jack Williams. He done his damndest."

"Whenever a man does the best he can," Truman told them, "then that is all he can do; and that is what your

President has been trying to do for the last three years for his country."

He returned to Washington with increased confidence. Democratic opposition to him disintegrated when Eisenhower firmly and finally bowed out of the race saying, "I will not at this time identify myself with any political party and could not accept nomination for any political office."

Truman then tried to persuade Supreme Court Justice William Douglas to be his vice-presidential nominee. Roosevelt had coupled Douglas and Truman as his 1944 choices for the vice-presidency. Douglas hesitated, then refused. But at the convention, Senator Alben Barkley made a rousing keynote speech to the delegates and was immediately mentioned as a vice-presidential possibility. Truman called him and said, "Why didn't you tell me you wanted to be Vice-President?" Earlier, knowing that Truman wanted Douglas, Barkley had told a friend, "I never cared for cold biscuits." But now he accepted.

Accepting the presidential nomination at two o'clock in the morning, Truman brought the delegates to their feet cheering when he said, "Senator Barkley and I will win this election and make these Republicans like it—don't you forget that."

It was a fighting speech ending with a dramatic piece of politics. After tearing into the "do-nothing" Eightieth Congress, Truman electrified the crowd by saying, "On the 26th day of July, which out in Missouri we call 'Turnip Day,' I am going to call Congress back and ask them to pass laws to halt rising prices, to meet the housing crisis, which they are saying they are for, in their platform." He then listed the Republican platform pledges.

"Now my friends," he said, "if there is any reality behind that Republican platform, we ought to get some action from a short session of the Eightieth Congress. They can do this job in fifteen days if they want to do it. They will still have time to go out and run for office. . . . What the worst Eightieth Congress does in its special session will be the test."

The American people, he said, "will decide on the record."

In his diary that night, Truman simply described the evening as "interesting and instructive."

What made it even more interesting was the walkout of thirty-five Southern delegates, who objected to the strong language of the civil rights plank. When a reporter interviewed the group's leader, Governor J. Strom Thurmond of South Carolina, and mentioned that Truman was only following the platform that Roosevelt had advocated, Thurmond said, "I agree, but Truman really *means* it." Two days later, Thurmond became the presidential nominee of the southern States Rights party, whose members were soon nicknamed "Dixiecrats."

The States Rights platform said, "We stand for the segregation of the races and the racial integrity of each race."

The sides were now set. The Republicans had again nominated, for the third time, Governor Thomas E. Dewey of New York. For his running mate, Dewey had picked Governor Earl Warren of California (who later became Chief Justice of the Supreme Court).

The Democrats were now split into three parts and three parties. Republican victory seemed so certain that the New York *Post* editorialized, "The Party might as well immedi-

152

ately concede the election to Dewey and save the wear and tear of campaigning."

Dewey had decided on a "high level" campaign that would not attack "the dignity of the office I was seeking." No name-calling, no "blood and thunder." He would give Truman the silent treatment. "My job is to prevent anything from rocking the boat," he said.

But Truman's plan was to name names and point fingers and rock all the boats.

To an audience of farmers, Truman said, "I spent all of my young days feeding cattle and livestock and hogs; so I know what I'm talking about on this." And then he pulled out a picture of Dewey and Warren standing next to a gate on Dewey's farm in upstate New York, and he pointed out that the gate was upside down. "That's how much Dewey knows about farming." But his clincher was the fact that the Republican Congress had voted against giving the Commodity Credit Corporation funds for grain storage bins. In a year of bumper crops and low prices, this had drastic meaning for farmers.

Dewey made the serious mistake of avoiding the farm issue. "There are some people who would like to inject politics into the necessities of food raising in our country. But I don't believe in that."

Dewey also didn't believe in too many speeches. Throughout the campaign he made forty-seven platform speeches and thirteen formal ones. A reporter wrote of Dewey, "He talked like a man who knew that the jury had made up its mind but simply wanted to give them a summing up." *Time* Magazine described opposition to Dewey because he seemed "too mechanistically precise to be liked . . . too coldly ambitious to be loved." Republican National Committeeman from Arizona, Clarence Buddington Kelland, later said, "The Dewey campaign was smug, arrogant, stupid and supercilious. . . ." On the other hand, Drew Pearson said, "As a technician, I would say Governor Dewey has conducted one of the most astute and skillful campaigns in recent years." *Newsweek* added, "The Dewey campaign is the accepted model of how a probable winner should conduct himself."

Dewey's main theme was "unity."

"Our people . . . yearn to move to higher ground, to find a common purpose in the fine things which unite us. . . . The unity we seek is more than material."

Truman hit that hard.

Slamming the Dewey team, he said, "They're using the farmer as a whipping boy in the cities and labor as the whipping boy on the farms. Apparently they figure that if they can get the city folk good and mad at the farmer and the farmer good and mad at the city folk, they will have unity."

His crowds got bigger. He spoke before one hundred thousand people in Seattle, and the police chief called it "the biggest crowd in thirty years." More and more now, he spoke without notes. "How many times do you have to be hit on the head before you find out what's hitting you? It's about time that the people of America realized what the Republicans have been doing to them. . . ."

". . . I'm not asking you to vote for me. Vote for yourselves! Vote for your farms! Vote for the standard of living that you've won under a Democratic administration! Get out there on Election Day and vote for your future!"

". . . If you place the government of this country under

the control of those who hate labor, who can you blame if measures are thereafter adopted that destroy the powers prestige and earning power of labor?"

Both labor and farmers got the message. Economically, the country seemed on the edge of trouble. The price of corn had dropped from $2.36 a bushel in January to a low of $1.38 by October 15. Postwar adjustment of industry had caused large pockets of serious unemployment throughout the country. More farmers now thought the government had forgotten them and more workers now feared the government had tied down their basic rights to strike. It had been predicted that labor would simply go through the motions for Truman—"slow motions." If they did at first, they soon switched signals. Most of labor steered clear of the Wallace Progressive party, because it seemed strongly tinged with Communists. Both the CIO and the AF of L each spent over a million dollars in support of Truman, pushed intensified registration drives on getting out the vote, including huge piles of pamphlets saying, "Don't strike out on Election Day!" They also hired cars to greet Truman at whistle stops, paid for speeches and spot announcements by the thousands on radio, and hired speakers to spread the Truman word.

As for the farmers, Louis Bean, an economist in the Department of Agriculture and a Truman friend, dressed as a chicken farmer and toured four midwest states conducting his own private poll. "I think you can win," he told Truman on his return. However, even Bean felt it would take a turnout of 60,000,000 votes to produce a Truman victory. Only 48,000,000 finally voted.

Truman's campaign funds were pitifully small compared to the Republican budget, and a reporter compared the two campaign trains as the "difference between horsehair and foam rubber." Thomas Stokes, another reporter, said that transferring from Truman's train to Dewey's was "like leaving a casual free-and-easy stock company on tour to join up with a slick New York musical."

Truman's "free and easy stock company" stopped moving several times "because we didn't have the money to pay the fare," Truman said. Once he called a wealthy Philadelphia friend from a railroad station to tell him that unless there was a certified check deposited the next morning for the railroad company, they would not permit his campaign train to continue. Truman's friend collected the money and paid the bill.

Truman's radio talks were cut short several times to dramatize his need for campaign funds. In one town he said, "The Republicans have the propaganda and the money. But we have the people, and the people have the votes."

Truman truly seemed to have the people. The crowds kept increasing at the whistle stops. On a rainy day in Albany, some 5,000 people came to greet the Truman train at eight o'clock in the morning. That same day 7,000 people came and stayed at the station in Auburn during a cloudburst. *Time* Magazine, commenting on the size and enthusiasm of the crowds, said, "Politicians and columnists are puzzled by the phenomenon."

Truman seemed to thrive on it. He traveled about 31,700 miles, delivered 356 speeches, averaging about ten speeches a day. On one single day, he gave sixteen speeches. His total audience was estimated at close to 15,000,000 Americans.

He mingled freely with the crowds, talked about his personal habit of being an early riser, told how much the area or people reminded him of Missouri, spoke about his daughter's graduation from college and said he called his wife "The Boss." Then he would say, "How would you like to meet my family?" Then Mrs. Truman and Margaret would come out and Margaret would throw a rose to the photographer when the train pulled out.

"I defy any reasonable person to meet Harry Truman and not like him," wrote reporter Richard Strout in *The New Republic*. "He is the kind of man who would make the ideal next-door neighbor—he would respect your rights, make allowance for your dog in his petunia bed, do thoughtful things for the family and shovel more than his share of the snow." Strout then added, "In spite of the ineptness, amateurishness and lack of organization which characterized the trip . . . these crowds are particularly enthusiastic."

"He stopped trying to be President," commented Joseph and Stewart Alsop in the New York *Herald Tribune*. "He's being Truman now."

But Truman could never stop being President, campaign or no campaign.

On the foreign front, Stalin had set up a blockade of West Berlin and refused to permit our supplies to pass through the Communist-controlled zone of Germany. We had promised to protect and supply this democratic piece of Germany which was surrounded by communism. Originally, the city had been put under the control of all four Allied powers after the war, but the Russians pulled out, after many arguments.

It was the kind of a situation that could explode into war. If we insisted on using force to bring in supplies past the

Communist zone of Germany, then war seemed inevitable. But Truman, against the advice of some of his military commanders, ordered the Berlin airlift. Using a continuous stream of our planes, with one landing almost every minute, we managed to supply the city with all its needs, and dramatized the power of our democracy to the whole world.

The success of this striking idea gave Truman's whole campaign an increased impact with the people.

Meanwhile Henry Wallace's Progressive party had run out of steam and support. His crowds had thinned out. The political power of the southern States Rights party was also still a large question mark, but the combination of both these fringe parties was still felt strong enough to fatally cripple any Truman hopes.

At least everybody else thought so—everybody except Harry Truman who felt completely confident of victory.

Newsweek Magazine polled 50 top political experts throughout the country and they gave Dewey 366 electoral votes, 100 more than he needed to win. All the other popular polls also gave Dewey a lopsided victory prediction. The Fort Lauderdale *Daily News* in Florida flatly announced that Dewey would get at least sixty-two percent of the vote.

Even some of Truman's closest friends, men who respected him highly and wished him the best, felt that his chances of winning were slim.

The press was so sure of the Dewey victory that they didn't even bother to hedge their bets. They prepared their election week issues, assuming that Dewey already had been elected.

Life Magazine featured a full-page picture of Dewey with

the caption, "The new President travels by ferryboat over the broad waters of San Francisco Bay." The *United States News* devoted fifteen pages of its election week issue to telling about the policies of the newly elected President Dewey. The *Kiplinger Letter,* already on the desk of leading businessmen, described the economic policies of the new Dewey administration. And *Manchester Guardian* correspondent Alistair Cooke wrote a final election story called, "Harry S. Truman—Study of a Failure."

On election night, Harry Truman was in Excelsior Springs, thirty-two miles from Kansas City. He took a Turkish bath, had a ham sandwich and a glass of milk, heard the early election returns which had put him slightly ahead, then went to bed early.

He awoke at midnight and listened to the radio broadcast of Mr. H. V. Kaltenborn. He was about 1,200,000 ahead on the count but, according to this broadcaster, was still undoubtedly beaten.

The Secret Service man woke him again at four in the morning and told him to tune in on Kaltenborn. "I did so," he said, "and learned at that time I was over 2,000,000 ahead, but the commentator continued to say he couldn't see how I could be elected."

Despite H. V. Kaltenborn, despite all the commentators and all the columnists and all the newspapers and all the polls who seemed so absolutely positive that he didn't have the remotest chance of winning, Harry S. Truman was still the elected choice of the people as their President of the United States.

Truman had 303 electoral votes, carried 28 states, Thurmond had 39 from four states, and Dewey had 189 from 16 states. Truman had 24,104,836 popular votes; Dewey, 21,-969,500; Wallace 1,000,000 votes.

"Labor did it!" said Truman. But he might also have given equal credit to the farm vote, and a good share to the Negro voters. Post election experts figured that a shift of 29,000 votes in critical states would have elected Dewey.

Truman was elated and gladly posed for a picture holding up a copy of the Chicago *Tribune* with the premature headline:

DEWEY DEFEATS TRUMAN

Returning to Washington, he saw a huge banner on the front of the Washington *Post* Building saying, "Mr. President, we are ready to eat crow whenever you are ready to serve it."

"When you win, you can't say anything," said Truman. "You're just happy. . . . Let's have no gloating." To his brother he said, "I just want to deserve the honor." To reporters he said, "Another four years of hard work ahead." For himself he wrote, "I wished that my mother had lived long enough to see me sworn in as an elected President."

HARRY TRUMAN WAS AGAIN SWORN IN AS
President of the United States.

In his inaugural address, he called on our country to lead
the democratic world, denounced communism, praised the
United Nations and pledged world peace as a major aim,
but said that this country would not shirk any fight with an
aggressor.

That morning he had a breakfast of country ham and
hominy grits with his old Army buddies of Battery D. When
one of them called him "Mr. President," Truman said, "We'll
have none of that here." After that, they all called him
Captain Harry. They were scheduled to march in the inaugural parade, and Truman told them:

"Although some of you have a rubber tire around the
middle, I'm sure you can still make 120 steps a minute for
a mile and a quarter." He also told them that he didn't
care what they did after the parade, "but I want you to stay
sober until then."

At his first post election press conference, Truman noted
that there were more reporters there than at any time during the campaign. Most of the correspondents were on the
Dewey Victory Special.

Asked whether it was true that it had been arranged for Truman to receive the electoral votes cast for Governor Thurmond, Truman's face stiffened and he said he didn't want the Dixiecrat votes. He'd won without New York, and without the Solid South, and he was proud of it.

But he never forgot he was a politician and a Democrat.

Long before, when the Washington *Post* editorialized that President Truman should appoint a lot of Republicans, Truman was asked about it at his press conference, and said, "I am a Democrat."

As for the rebel southern Democrats, or even Republicans, Truman had also said, "You know, I was a member of the Senate for ten years and found it didn't pay to fall out with a fellow because he was against you one time. The next time, when you needed him worse, you might be alone on your side."

"Politics and leadership are intertwined," he said. "A politician must be, in a sense, a public relations man. The best ideas in the world are of no benefit unless they are carried out. In order to carry them out, reason and persuasion must be employed. If enthusiasm for them can be aroused, so much the better. Some men have the ability to arouse that enthusiasm more than others. They are the political leaders."

He had aroused the people to enthusiasm during the election, but could he arouse Congress now?

At first the experts felt that Truman could get anything he wanted out of the newly elected Eighty-first Congress. But the Democratic House whip, Percy Priest, soon noted that more than a hundred of 263 Democratic Congressmen got more votes in their districts than Truman did "and they felt they didn't owe him a darn thing."

They acted that way, too. When Truman proposed his Fair Deal program of legislation, he listed twenty-four "must" proposals featuring a repeal of the Taft-Hartley Act, price control laws, liberalized immigration laws, minimum wage and a public housing law, among many other things.

He got a liberalized immigration law admitting more displaced persons, the war refugees without homes or countries —but he had to fight hard for it. He also saw his proposed law passed for low-cost public housing, but only because of the critical help given by Republican leader Senator Robert Taft.

Congress squelched most of his other proposals, including civil rights. On this, however, Truman used his presidential powers of executive orders to prevent racial discrimination in firms dealing with government contracts, which covered one fifth of the nation's economy. An executive order involved simply the signature of the President, and required no Congressional approval. He employed the same means to desegregate our armed forces.

He also kept up a continuous fight for his Point Four program.

Point Four was so called because it was the fourth point in his inaugural address—"to make the benefits of our scientific advances and industrial progress available for the improvement and growth of underdeveloped areas."

"I spend a lot of time looking at the map," said Truman, pointing to a globe of the world given to him by General Eisenhower, "and the more I look at it, the more I realize the possibilities of world development."

In answer to another question at another time, Truman said that the over-all purpose of Point Four was to help people to help themselves . . . make a beginning in providing instruction and assistance to each nation to develop its own resources.

Historian Arnold Toynbee predicted that Truman's Point Four program "will be remembered as the signal achievement of the age."

Congress didn't pass Point Four into law until June, 1950. Some 2,445 industrial experts and scientists were soon at work on more than a hundred projects in 35 countries. These were projects of health and sanitation, food supply, vocational education, projects to build dams and improve transportation of all kinds. Malaria was wiped out of pestholes in Peru and Burma, a typhus epidemic stamped out in Iran, school systems set up all over the underdeveloped world, a huge irrigation project started in Haiti, a giant hydroelectric plant in Mexico, 3,000,000 acres of Egyptian desert land transformed into a fertile farming area.

It was a program of help and a program of heart.

Truman now had a confidence nobody could smother. He had joked when the press criticized his idea for a balcony and building improvements for the White House. "I don't want to have to do what Dolley Madison was supposed to have done. They say she used to hang her washing in the East Room on rainy days." Later he added, "All changes in the White House since Fillmore's time have faced resistance—like gaslights and cooking stoves. Mrs. Fillmore put in the first bathtubs and she was almost lynched for doing it." Years later, in Independence, he showed a visitor at the Truman Library a piece of lumber in the basement. "Can you guess what this is?" he asked. The visitor couldn't guess. "This is the beam that gave way under Margaret's piano." It was that accident that caused a real renovation of the

White House. And it was Margaret's music that almost caused a mild social revolution. She was seriously preparing for a career as a concert singer. Truman, who never had trouble sleeping nights, said the only sleepless night he remembers was the one before Margaret made her debut.

His mother once described their family as a "touch-me-not" family "because we did not welcome intrusion on our private family affairs." Truman extended this definition. Critics could tear into him as much as they wanted, but he boiled if anybody criticized his wife or daughter.

When music critic Paul Hume of the Washington *Post* heard a Margaret Truman concert recital, he reported that she was "extremely attractive on stage" but that she could not sing very well and was "flat a good deal of the time."

Truman wrote an angry letter to Hume, saying that the review sounded as though it had been written "by an eight-ulcer man on a four-ulcer job, and all four ulcers working." He also added, "I never met you, but if I do, you'll need a new nose and plenty of beefsteak."

Friends blamed the letter on the strain of the presidential office. "Only the crises which Lincoln faced can be said to compare with the series of crises of today," said columnist David Lawrence. He referred to the constant crises caused by Communist expansion throughout the world.

When somebody circulated a rumor that Truman was in poor health, he said, "I never felt better in my life. I can take these Republicans on, one by one, with one hand tied behind my back. Don't worry about me!"

The ones who constantly worried about him were his Secret Service men, and with good cause. Take November 1, for instance.

A New York *Herald Tribune* headline splashed across the paper:

ATTEMPT TO ASSASSINATE TRUMAN IS FOILED: PUERTO RICAN PLOTTER SLAIN, SECOND WOUNDED: GUARD DIES, TWO SHOT IN BLAIR HOUSE BATTLE

TWO GUNMEN TRY TO SHOOT WAY TO PRESIDENT PENNSYLVANIA CROWDS SEE BATTLE: PUERTO RICAN NATIONALISTS ATTACK WHILE TRUMAN IS TAKING NAP

The weather was unusually warm for November, even reached eighty-four degrees, which made Washington particularly uncomfortable because of its dampness. President Truman had had a busy morning of meetings and conferences, and had awarded a Congressional Medal of Honor to a World War II marine hero for his exceptional bravery at Iwo Jima.

After lunch with his wife and mother-in-law, he went upstairs for a nap in the bedroom on the second floor at Blair House—across the street—where the Trumans were staying while the White House was being renovated.

It was 1:00 P.M. At 2:50 he was scheduled to make a speech at Arlington Cemetery.

At 2:20 two Puerto Ricans approached Blair House. There were guards on duty in white sentry boxes, and a White House policeman was also there, talking to a Secret Service man. Another policeman stood near the front door, where a canopy stretched to the sidewalk.

These two Puerto Ricans, Griselio Torresola and Oscar Collazo, both had guns and sixty-nine rounds of ammunition. They had come to kill President Truman, hoping that his murder would cause a revolution in this country during which time Puerto Rico would declare its independence of the United States.

It was so warm that the policeman had left the wooden door of Blair House wide open, but the screen door was still locked shut. Some people were quietly and quickly walking by the house when suddenly Torresola and Collazo rushed for the Blair House door. Before he had climbed two steps, Collazo was shot down. Within three minutes, thirty-one shots were fired—Torresola was killed and so was a White House policeman.

Truman had been stretched out on his bed when he heard the shots, and he ran and looked out of his window.

A policeman yelled at him, "Get back! Get back!" He quickly did.

The New York *Times* noted in an editorial that it all seemed especially senseless since Truman had appointed the first native ever to be governor of Puerto Rico and encouraged Congress to give Puerto Rico whatever status her people desired, including the right to vote for a constitution of their own creation.

If a President's day could be hectic, it could also be lonely.

"Had dinner by myself tonight," he once wrote in his diary. "Worked in the Lee House office until dinner time. A butler came in very formally and said, 'Mr. President, dinner is served.' I walk into the dining room in the Blair House. Barnett in tails and white tie pulls out my chair, pushes me up to the table. John in tails and white tie brings me a fruit cup. Barnett takes away the empty cup. John brings me a plate, Barnett brings me a tenderloin. John brings me asparagus, Barnett brings me carrots and beets. I have to eat alone and in silence in a candlelit room. I ring. Barnett takes the plate and butter plate. John comes in with a napkin and silver crumb tray—there are no crumbs but John has to brush them off the table anyway. Barnett brings me a plate with a finger bowl and doily and John puts a glass saucer and a little bowl on the plate. Barnett brings me some chocolate custard. John brings me a demitasse (at home a little cup of coffee—about two good gulps) and my dinner is over. I take a hand bath in the finger bowl and go back to work. What a life!"

Once he broke tradition by walking into the Senate chamber in the midst of a routine business day, took his old seat and sat there beaming like a schoolboy. Then he told his surprised colleagues, "I sometimes get homesick for this seat."

During a working day, he would sign his name on an average of six hundred times to various documents. His day would often begin at 5:30 A.M. and end at 11:00 P.M. He would have his breakfast, his walk, take care of his mail, see his staff at 10:00 A.M. This would include his three executive secretaries (appointments, correspondence and one for the press), the assistants to the President, his special counsel, three of his administrative assistants, his executive clerk and his three aides (military, naval and air). Each might bring up pending business, and he would hand each of them work to do.

He might then meet the National Security Council, concerned with the integration of domestic, foreign and military policies. Its executive director briefed him daily on world developments. Then there were always reports to read, a parade of people to see, some crisis needing his immediate attention.

"The presidential desk is like a general's," said Truman, "and it presents the same kind of problem . . . a leader is one who can persuade people to do what they don't want to do, and like it."

Truman confided to another reporter that the job of being President could break his back if he let it, but that he wouldn't let it. How could he help it? Simply by doing his best and not worrying about it, he said. He added that he supposed there were maybe a million people in the country who could do the job of President better than he could. But then he smiled and said that he was the one who had the job and so he was the one who had to do it. Talking to somebody else about the President's seventeen-hour working day, he again smiled and added, "but between you and me and the gatepost, I like it."

Perhaps the main reason he liked it was because of his deep sense of history. He knew that he had the power to help reshape the world. The continued threat to the peace of the world came from communism. Stalin's troops had moved into eastern Europe, completely controlled Hungary and Czechoslovakia. How could President Truman block this continued expansion without war?

His answer was the North Atlantic Treaty Organization, formed on April 4, 1949, and soon known as NATO. Twelve countries joined it immediately: Belgium, Canada, Denmark, France, Iceland, Italy, Luxembourg, the Netherlands, Norway, Portugal, the United Kingdom and the United States. Later, Greece, Turkey and West Germany also joined. Each country contributed its share of men and matériel into a single NATO military force to prevent any further Soviet aggression. With the consent of all the countries involved, General Dwight D. Eisenhower was proposed by Truman to be NATO's first supreme commander. Just as Truman's Marshall Plan had strengthened free Europe economically, and the Truman Doctrine strengthened it politically, his NATO proposal now gave free Europe a united military strength.

When Stalin saw himself stopped in Europe, he decided to probe elsewhere. He had already refused Truman's proposal of international control of atomic energy production. Truman had offered this plan to the world, through the United Nations, because he knew the horror of any future atomic war, and he wanted to guide the development of this enormous atomic force along peaceful lines. Stalin refused to accept the idea of inspection control.

Besides, Stalin had other aggressive ideas. The country of Korea had been split into two parts after World War II because Stalin had refused the postwar idea of a national election. Because of this, North Korea had become a Soviet satellite, supplied, equipped and directed by Soviet Russia. Stalin decided that now was the time to take over the whole country, using North Korean soldiers with Soviet guns and tanks. He judged that the United States would not intervene in such a remote country. He could then use a Communist Korea as a political springboard for further expansion throughout the Pacific.

But Stalin's judgment was wrong.

As a student of history, President Truman knew that if the free world permitted a Communist take-over of Korea, then it would be doing just what the League of Nations did when it failed to take action against Italy's invasion of tiny Ethiopia; it would be doing just what England and France did when they tried to appease Hitler at Munich by letting him take over Czechoslovakia. It was Truman's feeling that if the United Nations failed to act against this aggression now, it might never be able to act in the future. In that case the United Nations would die just as the League of Nations had died, and with it would die the hope of world peace.

It was not easy for President Truman to make the decision as Commander-in-Chief that would once again send American soldiers into battle. He himself knew what war was, the terror and the loneliness and the inhumanity of it. He had fought through one war and seen the incredible destruction of a second world war. And now he would have to be the one to order men to fight again. The way he saw it, we would either have to fight the Communists on a small scale to show that we were serious in our defense of the free world, or else we would have to fight them later on a much larger scale with many more casualties.

Truman saw this as the most important decision during his presidency.

He explained all this to the American people and they agreed with him.

So did General Douglas MacArthur, our Commander in Chief in that area. MacArthur said, "It was a historic decision which would save the world from Communist domination, and would be so recorded in history."

Our troops went to Korea, under the over-all mandate of

the United Nations. Soon there were troops from many other United Nations members fighting alongside the Americans.

Truman and MacArthur met at Wake Island on October 15, 1950, shortly after United Nations troops took the major offensive in driving back the North Koreans. He asked MacArthur about the possibility of Chinese troops intervening in Korea.

The general assured him that the victory was won in Korea. He also informed him that the Chinese Communists would not attack.

Back in Washington, however, the Central Intelligence Agency reported that as many as 200,000 Chinese troops had moved into Manchuria. Chinese planes soon were bombing our troops, flying back to their Chinese bases, and MacArthur wanted permission to bomb their bases in China. Truman and his top staff felt otherwise. "If we had gone ahead and bombed the Manchurian bases," said Truman, "we would have been openly at war with Red China and, not improbably, with Russia. World War III might very well have been on."

MacArthur started a major offensive to end the war, but Chinese troops did move into Korea and they beat back our offensive. MacArthur then felt that we should withdraw all our forces from Korea, or else face terrible losses—unless we were willing to go into an expanded war with China. The Joint Chiefs of Staff and National Security Council disagreed. MacArthur then released a statement expressing his disagreement with President Truman's decision not to expand the war into China.

President Truman regarded the MacArthur statement to

the press as an act of direct insubordination, still he took no action for two weeks. Then, however, Republican Representative Joseph Martin read aloud to the House of Representatives a private letter he had received from MacArthur, which repeated the criticism of the Truman policy in Korea.

Truman called a press conference on April 11, handed them an announcement which relieved General of the Army Douglas MacArthur of his command in the Far East, replacing him with General Matthew B. Ridgeway.

"He was insubordinate and I fired him," said Truman afterward, "just like Lincoln fired McLellan. . . . It was the right thing to do and I did it."

With the Korean War still on, there came the threat of a steel strike. Truman issued Executive Order 10340 for the government to seize and operate the 92 steel mills. "If steel production stops," he told the American people, "we will have to stop making shells and bombs that are going directly to our soldiers at the front in Korea. . . . I would not be faithful to my responsibilities as President if I did not use every effort to keep this from happening."

By a six-three decision, however, the United States Supreme Court ruled that our Constitution did not give the President the right to seize the steel industry.

This meant that the steel companies regained control of their mills, and the unions promptly went out on strike. It lasted seven weeks at an estimated cost of forty million dollars a day in production and wages. Truman finally permitted the companies to increase their price by five dollars and sixty-five cents a ton, and the strike was settled.

The time had come for another presidential election, another decision on whether or not to run again. The law, passed by the Republican Eightieth Congress, limiting the presidency to two terms did not apply to him since he had not served a full two terms. Besides, the law was written to begin with his successor. But Truman had long ago made up his mind.

When his friend and military aide, General Harry Vaughan, asked him, back in December, 1948, whether he was going to run again in 1952, he said, "Have you lost your mind? There is only one conceivable way I might be forced to and that is if we were right in the middle of a shooting war—which I don't think we'll be in."

On April 16, 1950, Truman had written himself a memo:

I am not a candidate for nomination by the Democratic Convention.

My first election to public office took place in November, 1922. I served two years in the armed forces in World War I, ten years in the Senate, two months and twenty days as Vice-President and President of the Senate. I have been President of the United States almost two complete terms.

Washington, Jefferson, Monroe, Madison, Andrew Jackson and Woodrow Wilson, as well as Calvin Coolidge, stood by the precedent of two terms. Only Grant, Theodore Roosevelt and F.D.R. made the attempt to break that precedent. F.D.R. succeeded.

In my opinion eight years as President is enough and sometimes too much for any man to serve in that capacity.

There is a lure in power. It can get into a man's blood just as gambling and lust for money has been known to do.

This is a Republic. The greatest in the history of the world. I want this country to continue as a Republic. When

Rome forgot Cincinnatus, its downfall began. When we forget the examples of such men as Washington, Jefferson and Andrew Jackson, all of whom could have had a continuation in office, then will we start down the road to dictatorship and ruin. I know I could be elected again and continue to break the old precedent as it was broken by F.D.R. It should not be done. That precedent should continue, not by a Constitutional amendment, but by custom based on the honor of the man in office.

Therefore, to re-establish that custom, although by a quibble I could say I've only had one term, I am not a candidate and will not accept the nomination for a third term.

When Truman announced this news at the annual Jefferson-Jackson Day dinner in Washington at the end of March, a silence came over the audience and then shouts of "No! No!" and then yells of, "We want Truman!"

But his decision was firm. His first choice for his successor was Chief Justice Fred Vinson, who declined because of a bad heart condition. Truman's next choice was the Governor of Illinois, Adlai Stevenson, a fresh face and a fresh voice in politics, a man who had been elected by more than half a million votes. Stevenson declined on the grounds that he had an obligation to the voters of his state to finish his term. However, a small group of amateur politicians in Illinois started a genuine draft of Stevenson and he finally consented to run.

Stevenson won the nomination, but lost the election by six million votes to General Dwight D. Eisenhower, who had decided to run on the Republican ticket. General Eisenhower's enormous popularity came from the fact that he had been a daily headline and a hero to the American people throughout the four years of World War II, when he led the Allied forces into Europe. During the campaign, Eisenhower had said, "I will go to Korea." Truman had attacked that as "cheap campaign tactics," and said, "Anybody who poses and talks like a superman is a fraud." This was the beginning of a bitterness between the two men.

The beginning of a coolness between Truman and Stevenson started when the latter told a reporter that he would clean up "the mess in Washington."

This was obviously a reference to the press attacks on Truman's old Missouri friends—the press called them "cronies"—who had supposedly taken advantage of their inside position at the White House to make huge profits on stock speculation, and to receive gifts for supposedly peddling their influence with the President. Truman, as always, remained loyal to his friends.

At his 324th and farewell press conference, 67-year-old Truman noted that he had taken 1,002 morning walks, that he had no plans on retirement but that he would never exploit the prestige of the presidency in anything he might do.

In his farewell address, Truman said:

. . . There is no job like it on the face of the earth—in the power which is concentrated here at this desk, and in the responsibility and difficulty of the decisions.

I want all of you to realize how big a job, how hard a job, it is—not for my sake, because I'm stepping out of it— but for the sake of my successor. He needs the understanding and help of every citizen. It is not enough for you to come out once every four years and vote for a candidate, and then go home and say, 'Well, I've done my part. Now let the new President do the worrying.' He can't do the job alone.

Regardless of your politics, whether you are a Republican or a Democrat, your fate is sealed up with what is done here in this room. The President is President to the whole country. We must all give him our support, as citizens of the United States. He will have mine and I want you to give yours.

He ended his farewell speech to the American people by saying, "I have tried to give it everything that was in me. . . . So as I empty the drawers of this desk, and as Mrs. Truman and I leave the White House, we have no regret. . . ."

In those final days just before he ended his second term in office as President, Harry Truman and Prime Minister Winston Churchill relaxed aboard the presidential yacht, the *Williamsburg*. Years before, when Truman became President at the death of Roosevelt, Churchill had said, "The day of the eagle is gone. The day of the sparrow has arrived." Now, as the two leaders of the free world sat across from each other at the dining room table, Prime Minister Churchill sipped his brandy, puffed at his cigar and said, slowly and dramatically:

"Mr. President, the last time we sat across a table together was at the Potsdam Conference in Berlin, and I must confess now that I held you in very low esteem."

Truman's friendly face grew grim.

"But now," said Churchill, "I must tell you that you and you alone saved western civilization from communism.

"When the Communists were knocking at the doors of

Greece, you and you alone made the decision to send the aid that saved that country from despair and destruction. When the Communists threatened to take over a devastated Europe, you and you alone provided the financial aid of America to save it with the Marshall Plan. When the Communists blockaded Berlin, you and you alone ordered the airlift of supplies to keep it alive. When the Communists threatened Afghanistan and the whole Middle East, you and you alone, Mr. President, provided the help it needed. And when the Communists threatened the freedom of Korea, and with it, the freedom of the whole Far East, you and you alone, Mr. President, made the decision to provide the strength to defeat it."

Churchill then lifted his brandy glass in a toast and said quietly, but with deep feeling, "I honor you, sir."

☆ ☆ ☆ ☆ ☆

WHAT DOES A PRESIDENT DO AFTER HE RETIRES from the presidency?

"There are a lot of people who would like to put a rock around them and throw them in the Potomac River," said Truman, smiling at the reporter who had asked the question.

More seriously, he added, "Every man who has held the presidency accumulates knowledge. It ought to be available for the welfare of the country."

Then he told New York *Times* reporter Cabell Phillips, "I might run for the Senate again when I'm ninety-one." Reporter Phillips added his postscript, "I'm not sure whether he was kidding or not."

Former Secretary of State Dean Acheson said of Truman, "Here is a man overflowing with life force, with incurable curiosity. He is no brooding image in a history book, depressed by the foibles and misfortunes of life; he is vigorous, powerful, gay, full of the zest of living. He is too much interested in what's ahead to deplore what is past."

"My only relaxation is work," said Truman, who doesn't hunt, fish or play golf, "and I have never known anybody to be injured by too much hard work. It is the lack of it that kills people."

179

He does most of his work in his office at the Truman Library in Independence, Missouri, a building built by public contribution and given to the government as a library of Truman's presidential papers. Truman's office there closely resembles his White House office.

"Well, I do like I always do," said Truman. "I get up early and begin the day by reading the New York *Times,* the *Herald Tribune,* the local papers and the St. Louis *Post-Dispatch.* Then I usually take a half hour stroll when the weather is good. Then I come on to the office and dictate anywhere from twenty to one hundred letters. The mail keeps coming, and it keeps three girls busy all the time answering it. After that, I meet the people who want to see me. They keep coming like they always did. I go to lunch around noon and come back in about an hour and a half. I finish the mail and look at the new mail. Late in the afternoon, I go home and look over the documents that are always piling up on my desk. I go over the drafts of my book, reading and editing. Outside of that, I don't have much to do."

He has written three books and is working on more. He also writes a syndicated column of opinion circulated in newspapers all over the country. He helps in fund-raising for all kinds of causes, including symphony orchestras, in one of which he played the piano in a duet with Jack Benny. "He's just a frustrated violin player," said Truman, "and I'm just a frustrated piano player."

And of course he appears at repeated fund-raising dinners for the Democratic party. "They treat me like I was a two-headed calf," he said laughing, "but if they want me to put on an exhibition, it's okay with me. The Democratic party has done a lot for me in my lifetime."

As a power in his political party, he was soon an outsider, as he knew he would be, but he still had a voice of bark and bite, and it was still a voice the party leaders listened to with respect. President John F. Kennedy often consulted with Truman on issues critical to the country, and so has President Lyndon B. Johnson.

The Trumans left their "rambling Victorian" eighty-nine-year-old house and toured Europe. Everywhere they were received with great warmth. Oxford College was one among many who gave Truman an honorary degree. In presenting the degree to "Harricum Truman," in Latin, Lord Halifax called him, "Truest of allies, direct in your speech and in your writings, and ever a pattern of simple courage." More informally, Halifax called Truman "the sort of person we would all be happy to go tiger-hunting with."

His daughter Margaret married New York *Times* editor Clifton Daniel on April 21, 1956. "I had always wanted a son," said Truman, "and now we have a grandson." His name is Clifton Truman Daniel. And soon there was another, William Wallace Daniel. When his grandchildren came to visit, said Truman, "There was no question who was in charge. They were."

Truman's interest in young people was much more than an interest, it had become the main purpose of his life.

"The surest way of showing you are arriving at the old-fogy class is to say that the young generation is going to the lower regions," said Truman. Later he added, wistfully, "It's a young man's age. It's the age of the greatest outlook.

181

Oh, how I wish I were eighteen years old. I wish I could go through this age with you, which you will face after I am gone. . . ."

"I think the rising generation has prospects before it that are really unequaled in the history of the world," he said. He had some words of warning, though, for the young people of America in their attitude toward the young people of Communist countries. "We must not return hate for the hate which these young people are being taught to feel toward us," he said. "We must realize that they are the victims of a sinful group of leaders. We must make it clear to them that we believe in the fellowship of human beings."

A student once asked him, "Mr. President, what is it you think of when you think of America?"

He answered:

"I think of America always in terms of people—people who are making this country what it is. . . . I think of Americans as the most generous people in the world. Whatever troubles or problems we face as a nation, I don't think there's anything to worry about regarding the heart of the American people, because it's in the right. We've taken the Irish, the Italians, the Jews, the Poles, the English and the French and the Germans, the Russians, the Swedes, the Norwegians, the Danes and the Greeks—and men and women from all parts of Europe and the world. And we've brought them together, and they are all Americans. . . ."

More than anything else, Truman said, he wanted to be known in history as "a people's President."

His good friend, Sam Rayburn, Speaker of the House of Representatives, said of Truman that he was "right on all the big things and wrong on all the little ones." Rayburn also told Truman, "Harry, history is going to be kind to you. They are going to forget the few times that you have not taken dead aim, but have shot from the hip. They are going to remember you for the great things you have done."

Truman once received a scroll from the National Press Club for being a "good public servant." He repeated the words, "good public servant," and added, "I hope that will be my epitaph."

SUGGESTED FURTHER READING

Abels, Jules. *Out of the Jaws of Victory.* New York: Henry Holt & Co., 1959.

Daniels, Jonathan. *The Man from Independence.* Philadelphia: J. B. Lippincott Co., 1950.

Helm, William P. *Harry Truman: A Political Biography.* New York: Duell, Sloan and Pearce, 1947.

Hillman, William. *Mr. President.* New York: Farrar, Straus and Young, 1952.

McNaughton, Frank and Hehmeyer, Walter. *This Man Truman.* New York: Whittlesey House, 1945.

Mason, Frank. *Truman and the Pendergasts.* New York: Regency, 1963.

Smith, A. Merriman. *Thank You, Mr. President!* New York: Harper & Bros., 1946.

Steinberg, Alfred. *The Man from Missouri.* New York: G. P. Putnam's Sons, 1962.

Truman, Harry S. *Memoirs: Year of Decision* (Vol. 1), *Years of Trial and Hope,* 1946-52 (Vol. 2). Garden City: Doubleday & Co., 1956.

——. *Mr. Citizen.* New York: Bernard Geis Associates, 1960.

INDEX

186

About the Author

RALPH G. MARTIN was born in Chicago and now lives with his family in East Norwich, New York. A graduate of the University of Missouri School of Journalism, he has been a newspaper reporter and was a combat correspondent during World War II. He turned to writing books after the war, concentrating his efforts on biography, politics, history. He has been a contributor to most of the national magazines, served as a consultant on "The Valiant Years," the TV documentary about Winston Churchill, and later became a magazine editor. He has also written fiction and is currently working on a play based on his first novel.

Photo by *Ed Wergeles*

About the Author

RALPH G. MARTIN was born in Chicago and now lives with his family in East Norwich, New York.

A graduate of the University of Missouri School of Journalism, he has been a newspaper reporter and was a combat correspondent during World War II.

He turned to writing books after the war, concentrating his efforts on biography, politics, history. He has been a contributor to most of the national magazines, served as a consultant on "The Valiant Years," the TV documentary about Winston Churchill, and later became a magazine editor. He has also written fiction and is currently working on a number of projects, among which are a play based on his first novel, a TV series and a second novel.